np

H. V

'S

ected boo
uctivit
).

)4-68

THE BENCHMARKING WORKBOOK

Adapting Best Practices for
Performance Improvement

THE BENCHMARKING WORKBOOK

Adapting Best Practices for Performance Improvement

Gregory H. Watson

Foreword by Carla O'Dell

Publisher's Message by
Norman Bodek

Productivity Press
Cambridge, Massachusetts   Norwalk, Connecticut

Productivity Press
P.O. Box 3007
Cambridge, Massachusetts 02140
United States of America
Telephone: (617) 497-5146
Telefax: (617) 868-3524

Cover design by Gary Ragaglia
Printed and bound by BookCrafters
Manufactured in the United States of America on acid-free paper

Library of Congress Cataloging-in-Publication Data

Watson, Gregory H.
    The benchmarking workbook : adapting best practices for performance improvement / Gregory H. Watson ; publisher's message by Norman Bodek.
        p.   cm.
    Includes bibliographical references and index.
    ISBN 1-56327-033-1 (acid-free paper)
    1. Organizational effectiveness.   2. Performance.   3. Business intelligence.
4. Competition--Evaluation.   I. Title.
HD58.9.W38 1992
658.4--dc20   92-4044
                                                                          CIP

10 9 8 7 6 5 4 3 2 1 92 93 94

To Joelyn with respect, gratitude, and love.

Contents

Publisher's Message

During the last decade, a total quality management surge swept through manufacturing and service industries in the United States. Companies learned the power of TQM principles to improve the way they served their customers and ultimately their competitive results. Continuous improvement of processes and products was a basic quality-management approach pursued by many companies.

For many organizations, however, continuous improvement has not led to the benefits expected. Companies spend valuable time and resources improving insignificant things without gaining a measurably better competitive standing, or they throw great effort into changes that aren't necessarily improvements at all. They need a solution that merges strategic choices about what activity to be good at with careful examination of what it means to be truly excellent in that activity. Benchmarking is that solution.

Companies that aspire to world-class status today cannot achieve it without benchmarking. Benchmarking is an effective TQM approach for guiding the improvement process by determining the most important things to improve and the best approaches for doing so. In its most basic definition, it is a methodology for determining the best practices in other organizations that will lead to superior performance in your company. Benchmarking, as Greg Watson says in the Introduction to *The Benchmarking Workbook*, "is a process for measuring your company's method, process, procedure, product, and service performance against those companies that consistently distinguish themselves in the same category of performance." The companies you will seek out for comparison are not necessarily your competitors, but organizations that you select for their superior results in your "key business processes" — the processes in your business that are most important because they directly or indirectly influence the external customer's perception of the company. The most famous example of this noncompetitive benchmarking is Xerox's study of L. L. Bean's warehousing and shipping process.

Many quality-minded managers today have heard of benchmarking and are aware of its benefits, but don't know how to begin. Greg Watson, formerly director of Corporate Quality at Compaq Computer Corporation, is an expert on the benchmarking approach. His *Benchmarking Workbook* is designed to give a basic understanding of benchmarking and to walk you through the basic steps of conducting a process benchmarking study, from determining what to measure to implementing process improvements in your workplace. To illustrate how to apply the concepts, each chapter is accompanied by a continuing case study adapted from an actual benchmarking case. Helpful forms are supplied throughout the workbook; full-page blank copies are reprinted in an appendix for convenient use during your own benchmarking study. Watson's thorough bibliographic references offer a ready resource if you want to pursue further study.

Benchmarking can be applied in many different contexts, as Watson describes in his Introduction. The facet of benchmarking most useful from a continuous improvement standpoint is process benchmarking — a method that focuses on discovering the best practices for conducting your company's key business processes, such as product design, claims processing, fabrication, or customer service.

Robert C. Camp's 1989 book, *Benchmarking*, brought this powerful tool to the awareness of quality-minded managers across the country. *The Benchmarking Workbook* builds on the foundation laid by Camp's book, offering a practical guide that will help you get started in process benchmarking. It presents the stages of a benchmarking study in six clear steps that correlate with the familiar TQM improvement cycle: Plan - Do - Check - Act (PDCA). The Introduction creates a context for understanding the purpose of benchmarking and its relation to a company's strategic plan and other forms of competitive analysis. Chapter 1 provides working definitions of the basic concepts used in process benchmarking. It shows you how to determine your company's core competencies and key business processes, as well as the critical success factors that measure the level of excellence in meeting customer needs, such as reliable quality, competitive cost, or short cycle time.

Chapters 2 through 7 address each of the six steps of the process benchmarking model. Careful attention is given in Chapter 2 to the planning stage.

Understanding your own organization and process and the reason for your benchmarking study is the essential foundation for everything else; this chapter assists you in clarifying and measuring the way you do things now.

Chapter 3 is about doing your homework. Too many organizations fall prey to the concept that benchmarking means visiting companies and asking questions. Before you get to the site visit stage, however, there is some serious research to be done. A wealth of information is available in the open literature. Watson assists by suggesting various sources for information gathering and offering forms for assembling the information into a useful comparison with what you've learned about your own processes.

Chapter 4 gets to the site visit. Watson describes the things to consider as you develop an information-sharing relationship with a benchmarking partner. Among the items covered are how to develop an effective questionnaire, how to shape questions appropriately, how to deliver them at the site visit, and how to record data gathered. Effective benchmarking requires the careful building of an environment of trust, cooperation, and learning between organizations. To help promote that mutual respect, the workbook offers legal and ethical guidelines for use of shared information.

Chapter 5 is about what you do when you get home from the site visit. The information you gathered must be used to have an effect. The material describes how to evaluate the information to discover the "performance gaps" between the the benchmarker's process and your own and the process differences that account for the gap.

Chapter 6 deals with figuring out how to adapt the superior practices you've discovered to the environment of your own organization. Watson leads the reader through development and implementation of an action plan, with consideration of practical issues such as getting necessary buy-in.

Chapter 7 is about the "act" stage of putting in place the process improvement you've adapted to your company's needs and tracking the results. Like the PDCA cycle, it doesn't stop there, but goes back to the beginning to review and plan further improvements.

Chapter 8 wraps up the book with a look at benchmarking itself as a process within the company and types of support that must be given for it to become an integral element of an organization's strategy and culture.

To succeed, benchmarking must become a companywide process. Top management must be involved in determining what is strategically important to improve. Cross-functional teams must do the work of discovering what their process is and learning how it could be better. Last but not least, the input of the people who will implement the improvement and live with it every day must be included during the entire process. To put the task of coordinating this effort into perspective, consider the true costs of trying to make changes *without* strategic corporate direction, outside information, and full buy-in from all employees.

The Benchmarking Workbook is an easy-to-read guide that will help managers sort out what is important to their customers and their company, learn how those things can be done better, and integrate that learning into their processes. It should be required reading for every executive, manager, and team member involved in benchmarking activities.

We at Productivity Press appreciate the opportunity to work with Greg Watson on this and the forthcoming books in his TQM series. Thanks also to Dr. Carla O'Dell, director of the International Benchmarking Clearinghouse, for contributing a wonderful foreword to this volume.

A number of Productivity Press staff members deserve recognition for their work on this volume. Our thanks to Dorothy Lohmann for managing the editorial process, with assistance from Laura St. Clair; to David Lennon and Gayle Joyce for production management, typesetting, and art preparation, and to Gary Ragaglia for the cover design.

Norman Bodek
President

Karen Jones
Series Editor

Foreword

Benchmarking burst onto the quality scene about three years ago. Widespread interest was fueled by benchmarking requirements in the Malcolm Baldrige National Quality Award criteria and further propelled by the outstanding examples of Xerox, Motorola, AT&T, and other early practitioners.

Benchmarking is getting lots of attention, but few companies as yet know how to do it well. A recent survey of International Benchmarking Clearinghouse member companies confirmed this situation: everyone agreed that benchmarking was critical for success. Unfortunately, 98 percent thought most companies did not have a clue how to do it.

Benchmarking is the process of understanding what is important to your organization's success, understanding your own processes, finding and learning from others who do these processes better than you do, then adapting that learning to improve your own performance. As with any new disciplines, benchmarking needs skilled communicators who can provide a framework for understanding how it builds on known disciplines and yet breaks new ground. Robert Camp and others of Xerox have made an enormous contribution to this. Now, with this workbook, Greg Watson takes the process another step.

Greg plants benchmarking firmly in the quality discipline and its quest for customer satisfaction and continuous improvement. When done well, benchmarking draws on the existing knowledge and tools of strategic planning and competitive analysis, process analysis and improvement, team building, data collection, and, perhaps most important, change management.

Benchmarking sounds eminently logical and is quite appealing, but many barriers exist to doing it well. The greatest contribution of this book is the help it provides in overcoming the barriers to effective benchmarking.

Barriers

We as Americans have a lot of psychological baggage to discard before we can successfully learn from others. Perhaps the greatest is the fear of being seen as "copying." From kindergarten onward, we have been punished for working together and rewarded for individual achievement.

Breakthroughs come from understanding what has gone before, then surpassing it. Sir Isaac Newton clearly understood this when he said, "If I have seen further, it is because I have stood on the shoulders of giants." What greater compliment can the student pay the teacher than to surpass him or her?

Benchmarking is far more than copying. It requires deep self-assessment, and the ability to translate practices that work in another context into a process appropriate to your own organization. It is the essence of creativity.

Second only to the fear of being seen as a "copycat" is the fear of losing competitive advantage by sharing information. As Greg points out, few organizations would, or should, share competitive or proprietary information with competitors or unauthorized others. But the realm of proprietary advantage is quite small. Those islands of competitive advantage are surrounded by oceans of opportunity in business and management processes. Competitive advantage is in speed and quality of execution and deployment, not information.

New benchmarkers are always astonished (and humbled) by other practitioners' willingness to share. It is remarkable how willing people, especially those involved in the quality movement, are to share their success stories. They are proud of what they do.

This raises the central importance of ethics and clear expectations, treated so well here. The Clearinghouse is possible only because its participants subscribe to a code of ethics that eliminates many of the concerns that keep people from sharing. One of the principles is that of "reciprocity": do not ask others to tell you things you would not be willing to reciprocate with the same level of information.

The third barrier is arrogance. "We are the best. Why benchmark?" In response, Greg asks the classic Deming question: "How do you know?" How do you know you are so good if you never compare your processes to those of others?

Benchmarkers who follow Greg's advice will not step into the fourth trap that lies in wait for them — the trap of benchmarking that which is convenient but may be unimportant. Knowing what to benchmark is at least as important as knowing how to benchmark. Every organization has those few things it must do well in order to compete and thrive — its "core competencies." These are key processes that contribute most strongly to customer satisfaction and quality assurance in both the short and long term. As Greg articulates so well, benchmarking without first understanding strategy is a waste of precious limited resources.

It is also fragile. Benchmarking not tied to strategy can be vulnerable to failure, a lesson painfully learned by the early practitioners of employee involvement. Employees were certainly involved, just not in anything really critical. They were working on problems of little significance to customers, quality, or the future of the firm. Employees complained that management lost interest. The truth is that employees were still relegated to the sidelines of competitiveness.

The fifth issue in benchmarking is impatience, a quintessential American trait. Action always has more appeal than planning. Do something, anything. As a result, benchmarking too often consists of "industrial tourism." On any given day, hundreds of groups of managers are walking through someone else's plant or office, asking questions as they occur to them, expressing delight and appreciation at what they see, and going home. Interesting? Yes. Entertaining? Almost always. Productive? Only if you are lucky.

But it's a far cry from the deep analytical work that needs to be done to really adapt and adopt those practices to your situation. It takes time to do it well. This book provides the process and the tools to effectively plan and deploy a benchmarking study. Without this planning, the benchmarking project will result in frustrated people and lackluster results.

This workbook also helps by providing a simple process and the tools to speed the planning and preparation. The benchmarking team will find here the tools and forms to support the process, make it more efficient and more likely to lead to information that will be used for improvement.

The final and worst benchmarking mistake is not doing it at all. We have heard all the excuses. "We are too small." "We are too busy." "We are different; no one does what we do." "We do it better than anyone else." Why benchmark? Greg Watson argues persuasively against each of these excuses.

Accelerating the rate of improvement is the key competitive issue facing organizations. By exposing the need for change, quantifying the magnitude of the improvement needed, and modeling an example of how it can be done, benchmarking can enable quantum leaps in improvement.

Through this workbook Greg Watson makes a major contribution to the discipline of benchmarking. I am sure the dedicated reader will benefit as much from this book as I did from having the author as a colleague during its genesis.

Carla O'Dell, Ph.D.
Director, International Benchmarking Clearinghouse
American Productivity and Quality Center

Preface

To remain in ignorance of the enemy's condition, simply because one grudges the outlay of a hundred ounces of silver in honors and emoluments, is the height of inhumanity.

— Sun Tzu

LIVING IN CHAOS

In 1989 I lived in Loma Prieta, California. Loma Prieta is known as the epicenter of the major San Francisco earthquake of October 17 of that year. During the week following the earthquake there were over 100 aftershocks, many of them over 5.0 on the Richter scale. Walking in that area felt like surfing on liquid ground. The paradigm of solid earth had failed. Many of the residents of that small community could not take this change and moved away.

In the emerging theory of chaos, the metaphor of white water is used to express the phenomenon of continuously fluctuating reality.[1] The volatility of our current business situation is a wonderful example of this chaos. Turbulence is born of economic, political, social, or technological events and erupts into disintegrating order in the business realm. Order disintegrates into disorder and then this chaos gives birth to a new model of order.

Business needs to cope with this change in real time, learning to live with the disorder that is presented to it. This is similar to learning to paddle a canoe through white water. There is always the possibility of wrapping that canoe around a slightly submerged rock. The person paddling in the bow has the responsibility to look ahead and apply a correcting bow rudder to avoid these obstacles that are not visible from the stern, where a canoe is steered in calmer waters. Applying the bow rudder is a technique that business needs to learn in order to be able to make rapid corrections in its course through the white water.

APPLYING THE MILITARY METAPHOR

In military science, the United States has developed a world-class capability to look ahead through this white water. By applying the combination of good intelligence with computer simulation and war gaming theory, the military is able to project the various potential threat conditions and "play" them through at their war colleges, years in advance of the real situation. The American success in Operation Desert Storm is an example of the military's farsightedness. In the early 1970s, officers played war games around the Iraq-Iran theater, probing the many possibilities of warfare in this strained political atmosphere and turbulent environment.

Throughout this book, I have provided quotes from Sun Tzu and Miyamoto Musashi, two ancient oriental military strategists who guide the current thinking of the American military.[2] They provide the basis for "commercial warfare" theory in Japanese business. From the perspective of military science, good intelligence is fundamental to conducting a campaign. Benchmarking is a business tool for helping to understand and anticipate the potential moves of competitors. After management learns to successfully capture process improvement information through benchmarking, then simulation and game theory may provide interesting next steps for new business improvement tools.

MANAGING CHANGE EFFECTIVELY

The open sharing of information about business practices is one of the more exciting aspects of the current American quality movement. This sharing transcends the natural boundaries of competition and trade barriers. Companies are becoming learning organizations, and a principle tool for this learning is benchmarking. Benchmarking is a structured approach to gaining information that will help your organization anticipate the white water and improve its ability to steer through the business environment.

Dr. W. Edwards Deming has observed: "I think people here [in the United States] expect miracles. American management thinks that they can just copy from Japan. But they don't know what to copy."[3] Effective benchmarking links the desire to learn from other companies with the need to strategically allocate an organization's resources. By linking benchmarking with strategic planning, organizations can focus their change-management ability on the areas that will provide the highest payoff in terms of quality, productivity, and customer satisfaction. Although benchmarking was developed as a quality tool in Japan, it was introduced to American business by Xerox in the mid-1970s.

THE XEROX CONTRIBUTION

Benchmarking has become widely accepted as a useful quality tool, due much to the success of the early pioneers from Xerox who began benchmarking by conducting studies as early as 1976. The Xerox benchmarking process began in the copier duplicator manufacturing division. Frank Pipp, vice president for the division at the time, is considered by many at Xerox to be the executive champion and driver for the development of this practice. Indeed, he is sometimes called the "father of benchmarking" in recognition of his leadership support. Early members of these benchmarking efforts include Norm Ricard, Bob Strosser, and Steve Snow.

Pipp was subsequently promoted to senior vice president for copier duplicator development and manufacturing; he continued to drive the benchmarking effort with an engineering focus through Frank Regensburger, Art Tweet, Mohan Kharbanda, Bruce Lippa, and Dev Khanna. Benchmarking then spread to other areas of Xerox and involved John Kelsch, Paul Sawicki, Bob Camp, Jack Kelly, Peter Connelly, and Cary Kimmel.

A significant event happened when Tom Barchi, on loan from the General Accounting Office, interviewed the Xerox benchmarking practitioners and edited their methods into the *Red Book*, the accepted companywide benchmarking practice. Bob Edwards and Jules Cochoit subsequently developed the pilot training program. Bob Camp documented the Xerox best practice in his book, *Benchmarking: The Search for Industry Best Practices That Lead to Superior Performance*.[4]

There were undoubtedly many other individuals who made significant contributions to Team Xerox for benchmarking and to whom we owe our gratitude. To all of these individuals, I express my appreciation for pioneering the development of this methodology and preserving the lessons learned as they successfully turned around their business. Benchmarking has become one quality tool with a value that is easily appreciated by those outside the professional quality community.

NETWORKING AS AN INTERNATIONAL NEED

There is an imperative in strategic planning: that we know where we stand today relative to our competitors and to our virtual competitors. We know our current competitors, but our virtual competitors include any company that has the ability to take advantage of technological, economic, legislative, or regulatory changes to create a product or service that directly competes with our own. This means that we must study other businesses on a regular basis. Thus, the planning of a business must be tied closely to the use of benchmarking as an analytical tool of business strategy.

The need for networking and continuous learning has been the topic of several recent books.[5] One vehicle for continuous learning is the International Benchmarking Clearinghouse (IBC) service of the American Productivity and Quality Center (APQC). Through the farsightedness of Dr. C. Jackson Grayson, Carla O'Dell, and Marty Russell, nearly 90 companies have banded together to develop a vision: to improve productivity and quality in organizations throughout the world by promoting, facilitating, and improving the application of benchmarking.[6]

The IBC is a model organization for networking among businesses. The mission of the clearinghouse is to be a networking organization, a repository of benchmarking information, a gateway to information in other organizations, and a center of expertise for benchmarking know-how, and to continuously refine, develop, and promote the benchmarking process. Although the clearinghouse is located in the United States and serves American businesses, it is international in scope, believing that the improvement of productivity and quality is a win-win situation for all nations.

I have elected to help APQC establish the clearinghouse because I believe that we need a strong national focus to improve the competitive position of American business. A concerted effort by American companies can help stimulate the environment needed by promoting benchmarking activities on an international level.

Gregory H. Watson

NOTES

1. John Briggs and F. David Peat, *Turbulent Mirror: An Illustrated Guide to Chaos Theory and the Science of Wholeness* (New York: Harper and Row, 1989), have produced a readable introduction to chaos theory and its application in science.

2. Miyamoto Musashi, *The Book of Five Rings,* trans. Victor Harris (Woodstock, N.Y.: Overlook Press, 1974); Sun Tzu, *The Art of War,* ed. James Clavell (New York: Delacorte Press, 1983).

    In *The Book of Five Rings*, Musashi described the way of strategy using nine broad principles:

    1. Do not think dishonestly.
    2. The way is in training.
    3. Become acquainted with every art.
    4. Know the ways of every profession.
    5. Distinguish between gain and loss in worldly matters.
    6. Develop intuitive judgment and understanding for everything.
    7. Perceive those things which cannot be seen.
    8. Pay attention even to trifles.
    9. Do nothing which is of no use.

    These principles apply to the attitude of individuals participating in benchmarking. While Musashi was teaching the art of samurai warfare, he addressed competitive behavior in general. For instance, he commented that "if you are thoroughly conversant with strategy, you will recognize the enemy's intention and thus have many opportunities to win."

    The military model has been adapted to business as the "art of commercial warfare." Musashi encouraged his followers to "become the enemy." This means that you "think yourself into the enemy's position." These basic principles of warfare apply to benchmarking other companies. This thesis underlies the strategic application of benchmarking as a quality tool. Benchmarking was also a tool that the Japanese used to become recognized as "masters of imitation" in the 1950s through 1970s. Perhaps we have some lessons to learn by benchmarking their strategic principles.

3. Quoted by Mary Walton, *The Deming Management Method* (New York: Perigee Books, 1986), 18-19.

4. Robert C. Camp, *Benchmarking: The Search for Industry Best Practices That Lead to Superior Performance* (Milwaukee: Quality Press/Quality Resources, 1989).

5. Charles M. Savage, *Fifth Generation Management* (Maynard, Mass.: Digital Press, 1990), and Peter M. Senge, *The Fifth Discipline: The Art and Practice of the Learning Organization* (New York: Doubleday Currency, 1990), propose the significance of the networking model and the continuously learning organization.

6. One of the first contributions of the IBC was the development of a proposed standard definition of benchmarking.

> Benchmarking is the process of continuously comparing and measuring an organization with leaders anywhere in the world to gain information that will help it to take action to improve its performance. Competitive benchmarking is benchmarking organizational performance against performance of competing organizations. Process benchmarking is benchmarking discrete processes against organizations with performance leadership in those processes.

> IBC published these definitions as a formal benchmarking guideline in the first quarter of 1992.

Acknowledgments

I want to take this opportunity to acknowledge the influences on my motivation to write this book. First, I would like to thank my father, Robert J. Watson, a newspaperman, who taught me the value of expressing my thoughts in written word. I would also like to thank my mother, Anne B. Watson, a schoolteacher, who taught me the value of continuous learning. My son, Andy Watson, has taught me the importance of unbridled creativity. My twin brother, Jeffrey B. Watson, has taught me that there are many paths to happiness. My cousin, Ethel Baker, has shown me that there is much wisdom yet to be learned in life. I would like to thank Jack Grayson for the encouragement to express these thoughts in writing and Karen Jones of Productivity Press for helping to drive this work into publication. Finally, I would like to thank my wife, Joelyn Brandon Watson, for her encouragement through what began as friendship and grew into love. Thank you all.

Introduction
Benchmarking for Continuous Improvement

The Business Environment
- The Business Environment
- Benchmarking Defined
- Competitive Analysis

About Process Benchmarking

The highest form of generalship is to balk the enemy's plans; the next best is to prevent the junction of the enemy's forces; the next in order is to attack the enemy's army in the field; and the worst policy is to besiege walled cities. . . .

— Sun Tzu

Continuous improvement and customer satisfaction are the two basic principles of total quality management (TQM). To effectively execute TQM, a company should focus on these two business fundamentals; however, it is not evident in what area a company should focus its continuous improvement effort to achieve higher levels of customer satisfaction. That's where benchmarking comes in.

Your business competitors are also focusing on continuous improvement to achieve higher levels of customer satisfaction. Gaining an advantage over competitors is the mission of benchmarking. This workbook provides a practical example for applying this method to your business to improve your company's competitive position. The complementary textbook explains one theory for applying competitive business practices and position benchmarking relative to other competitive practices.[1] This workbook provides the information needed to initiate, plan, and develop your benchmarking efforts, while the textbook provides the knowledge for integrating benchmarking with market research, competitive intelligence, industry analysis, product positioning, and reverse engineering.

The workbook tracks the benchmarking process and uses a case study to demonstrate how each step in this process is applied. Please feel free to use the forms to help you conduct your benchmarking projects; they are reprinted in the Appendix for your convenience.

Some introductory remarks will help set the stage for the benchmarking process used in this workbook. This introduction summarizes the textbook's thesis and establishes its connection to the benchmarking process.

THE BUSINESS ENVIRONMENT

The competitive climate of a business enterprise can be described using a model proposed by Larry Miller.[2] A business is challenged by forces of change from without and within its own boundaries. Each business system is composed of a set of processes that deliver its products or services to its customers. Changing the business system can be motivated by internal pressures from the leadership of the organization, for example, by changing the vision, mission, or goals of your company. Change can also be motivated by external forces as a function of your company's legislative, regulatory, political, social, economic, technological, or competitive situation. A simplified version of Miller's model is presented in Figure 1.

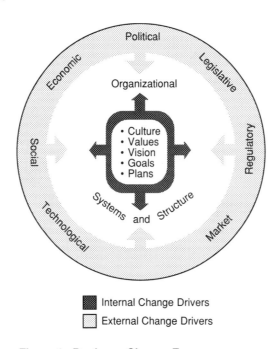

Figure 1. **Business Change Forces**

The internal change-driving force in your company must exceed the external change-driving force if your company is to stay in an industry leadership position. Miller states: "Corporations will compete successfully only if they have achieved a culture that promotes the behavior necessary for competitive success."[3] A part of this culture is the need to examine current performance trends to determine your competitive position.

Benchmarking is a tool that complements strategic planning to enhance your company's competitive position. By studying other companies and the methods that enable them to build ongoing business success, you can become better prepared to wage economic warfare.

BENCHMARKING DEFINED

Before discussing the strategic implications of benchmarking, it is important to define the term. Since benchmarking became popularized through Bob Camp's book, his general definition will be used: *the search for best practices that will lead to superior performance.*[4] Benchmarking is a process for measuring your company's method, process, procedure, product, and service performance against those companies that consistently distinguish themselves in that same category of performance. Thus benchmarking is a customer-driven commitment to continuous process improvement. This definition highlights the strategic importance of benchmarking.

A strategic view takes the broadest perspective of your business and compares your performance with your competitors to understand relative competitive advantages. Benchmarking provides an improvement strategy by seeking comparisons that go beyond the boundaries of your industry to find world-class best practices that are independent of the industry in which they are observed and that can be adapted to provide competitive advantage in your industry.

If you fall into the trap of making all comparisons against your competitors, you will find your company in a state of industrial paralysis where each competitor applies the same business paradigm. By seeking knowledge from outside your industry, you can develop innovative opportunities that create discontinuities with the accepted industry best practices. These best practices eventually cause stagnation by bringing all competitors to the same level of performance and eliminating market differentiation. If benchmarking is therefore focused only on competitors, it will not lead to superior performance.

BENCHMARKING AND STRATEGIC PLANNING

How should benchmarking be used in strategic planning? Benchmarking is a tool for setting appropriate measurable strategic objectives for business improvement milestones and targets. In the introduction to Yoji Akao's book, *Hoshin Kanri*, I suggest linking benchmarking with strategic planning.[5] Graphically, this linkage depicts current benchmarks and relates them to short-term goals. These current benchmarks are then projected from the current levels to establish competitive long-term goals. This scheme provides a rational approach for setting meaningful long-term goals. Figure 2 illustrates the relationships between these measures for a generic process critical success factor or performance measure.

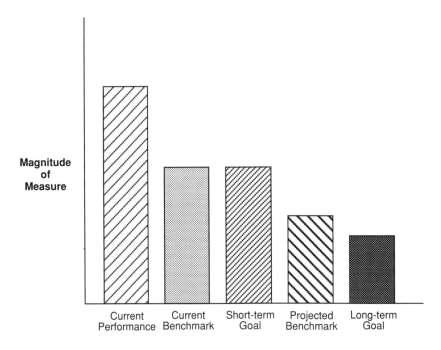

**Magnitude
of
Measure**

Current
Performance

Current
Benchmark

Short-term
Goal

Projected
Benchmark

Long-term
Goal

Figure 2. Benchmarks Applied to Planning Goals

Developing a benchmarking study plan that supports your strategic objectives with measurable performance targets is a productive way to integrate benchmarking into the strategic planning process. Strategic business improvement is gained by focusing on both short-term and long-term objectives. Short-term objectives tend to be incremental — *kaizen* — or continuous business improvement objectives. Long-term objectives are usually breakthrough — *hoshin* — or strategic business improvement objectives. Most managers learn to direct a project for the short term; however, the key to persistent business success is your company's ability to guide the long-term change process. Benchmarking is a quality tool that helps set the direction for long-term, strategic business improvement.

To attain enduring business success, both short-term and long-term objectives must be achieved. Benchmarking can help strategically focus your company's continuous process-improvement efforts by providing challenging, but attainable, goals that stretch your company's ability to perform. If another business can reach a benchmarked level of performance, then your company can, too.

If we accept that benchmarking can help formulate the direction of our strategic planning process, then we must understand how it fits into the set of competitive analysis tools that we already are using in our company.

COMPETITIVE ANALYSIS

Besides benchmarking, other analytical tools used for assessing competitive information may include industry analysis, product positioning, product reverse engineering, and service mystery shopping. The matrix in Figure 3 compares the primary competitive analysis methods and their related business quality focuses.[6] Perceived quality or customer-focused quality is a strategic management, or TQM, approach, and conformance quality or product-focused quality is a tactical management or quality assurance (QA) approach. Figure 3 illustrates the relationship between these tools and benchmarking.

A number of books are available to describe these approaches: My textbook, *Benchmarking for Competitive Advantage*, provides a design for using these competitive practices in concert with each other. The fundamental aspect of this design is the relationship between the strategic and tactical aspects of these tools in market-oriented and operations-oriented applications. Leonard Fuld's book, *Competitor Intelligence*, is the basic reference for the use of competitive information.[7] Michael Porter's works describe the market side of industry analysis and product positioning found in the competitive tools matrix (Figure 3).[8] Kaiser Associates, Inc., has produced a market-oriented guide to benchmarking.[9]

Focus	Market	Operations	Business Quality
Strategic	Industry Analysis	Benchmarking	Perceived Quality (TQM) Customer Survey
Tactical	Product Positioning	Reverse Engineering or Mystery Shopping	Conformance Quality (QA) Customer Complaint

Figure 3. Competitive Analysis Matrix

ABOUT PROCESS BENCHMARKING

This workbook focuses on *process benchmarking*. This form of benchmarking involves seeking the best practice for conducting a particular business process. Process benchmarking is not the only type of benchmarking; however, it is the form of benchmarking that can help improve your key business processes because it can adapt lessons from the best practices of companies that your research has determined to be the world leaders or trendsetters. Process benchmarking is a form of analysis distinct from other types of benchmarking: strategic, performance, competitive, tactical, functional, generic, and industry.

Companies that are not strategically focused tend to look at tomorrow's business much as they see today's. They make the mistake of failing to anticipate market trends and competitive moves that could continue to keep them active players in their industries. *Strategic benchmarking* helps avoid this situation because it focuses on the potential changes in a business by examining nonindustry companies for significant business trends. General Electric provides a good example of this type of benchmarking; having established benchmarking alliances with a limited number of noncompeting businesses and examining their trends over a long period of time. General Electric uses this partnership with fewer than 20 internationally recognized businesses to provide in-depth insights into specific change initiatives. These partnerships began with nine companies in the early 1980s and has been limited by choice to a small number of participating companies.

Industry and *competitive benchmarking* are similar in that they focus on industry-specific comparisons. Competitive benchmarking focuses on your company's direct competition, for instance, when two companies, such as Kodak and Canon, evaluate their relative positions for strategic manufacturing of the same product (e.g., copiers or cameras). Industry benchmarking takes a slightly broader view and targets companies with dissimilar products within the same industry. For example, if Kodak conducted a study of strategic manufacturing at an electrical equipment company such as Black & Decker.

Generic benchmarking occurs when a particular process or business function is evaluated against target companies regardless of their industry. The best-known example of this type is the Xerox study of L.L. Bean. *Functional benchmarking* compares a particular business function at two or more companies. *Tactical benchmarking* is when a process-focused team from one company compares one of their specific processes with "best of process" selected without regard to industry. In a functional benchmarking study, the targeted process is usually a key business process, whereas in a tactical benchmarking study the process need not be a key business process. (Chapter 1 distinguishes key business processes from others.)

Performance benchmarking measures the performance of one company's products or processes against those of another company. A good example is found in the computer industry where benchmark studies are used to see which computer runs faster while executing a standard test program. Stock analysts also perform benchmark studies to compare the relative financial performance of one company against others in its industry.

It is not evident how these forms of benchmarking fit into a clean taxonomy of study types. Indeed, they do not. For this reason, I prefer to use process benchmarking when referring to any study that looks at process-specific performance. This includes generic, functional, and tactical benchmarking as well as the examples of competitive and industry benchmarking.

A more helpful classification divides the types of benchmarking into categories relative to the actions required to support them. Using this approach, I divide benchmarking into three categories: strategic, performance, and process.

Using these classifications, strategic benchmarking reflects the General Electric model for long-term, noncompetitive alliances. Performance benchmarking describes all research-based studies of competitors and industry participants that are based on the analysis of trends through database interrogations and surveys. Process benchmarking refers to those studies that result in face-to-face observation of the targeted or key business processes, regardless of which type of company is targeted as "best practice" potential.

This way of categorizing benchmarking projects is helpful when allocating resources to meet your demand for information. For instance, strategic benchmarking requires a small professional team with long-term continuity. Performance studies, on the other hand, can be conducted by an experienced research-oriented librarian and a market research staff that specializes in surveys (perhaps augmented by consulting firms that specialize in within-industry or cross-industry surveys). Process benchmarking, moreover, requires the participation of subject matter experts. This implies that the owner of the process and the process team should be directly involved in conducting the study.

Figure 4 defines and contrasts these three types of benchmarking and the level of resources required to support each study in a balanced companywide program.

Type of Benchmarking	Definition	Support Resource Requirement
Strategic	The analysis of world-class companies in noncompetitive industries to determine opportunities for strategic change initiatives in core business processes. These studies are performed by professionally trained benchmark analysts.	Medium-Low
Performance	The analysis of relative business performance among direct or indirect competitors. These studies focus on open-literature analysis or are conducted as "blind" studies using a third-party consulting firm.	Low
Process	The analysis of performance in key business processes among identified best-practice companies selected without regard to industry affiliation. Studies are conducted by teams from process area.	High

Figure 4. Benchmarking Program Elements

This three-pronged approach to benchmarking allows your company to gradually build its benchmarking capability. You can start with performance benchmarking, which requires the least resources in terms of headcount. Then you can go on to build partnerships with a set of companies to understand strategic issues for your company. Some of the companies you can readily solicit to join your strategic benchmarking project might include your suppliers and major customers. These businesses have a vested interest in helping you stay competitive. Building your resource base through membership in some industry-specific studies and by using national data bases also improves the breadth of competitive information. (Leonard Fuld's book provides a good overview of secondary source information for your data needs.) Finally, as your company becomes more capable of adapting benchmarking information, you can begin a team-training program to help your process teams conduct their process benchmarking studies. Opportunities for process benchmarking studies naturally follow your involvement in strategic and performance benchmarking.

This gradual introduction of benchmarking to your company has definite advantages: It provides a low-resource approach to building your company's capability to benchmark while also building your company's credibility with more experienced benchmarking partners. In addition, by focusing first on the strategic and performance aspects of benchmarking, you also build the tools needed to support process benchmarking for your teams. Both strategic and performance benchmarking provide you with a low-overhead introduction to the organizational structure, resource requirements, legal aspects, and systems support needed for a formalized benchmarking process, and they also provide your company's management with an early introduction to the benefits of benchmarking.

Many companies ask: Why should we establish a formal process for conducting these benchmarking studies? Why can't we just visit those companies that we know are outstanding and learn our lessons quickly? Perhaps an anecdote from my experience will help explain.

Most companies seriously involved in benchmarking efforts (IBM, Xerox, Johnson & Johnson, 3M, Hamilton-Standard, Dow-Corning, Motorola, and General Electric, to name a few) are besieged with requests to participate in benchmarking studies. Many of the requesters have just begun their benchmarking efforts and are novices in conducting these studies. One such company (a *Fortune* 100 business) requested a benchmarking study with Compaq on a topic of strategic interest. After agreeing to participate in this study, I discovered that they had selected *only* our company to benchmark. Their initial research had not turned up any other company to compare against us! They submitted a list of 57 questions they hoped to cover in a four-hour, face-to-face session—this boils down to only four minutes per response with no time allowed for discussion.

Contrast this inexperienced approach with that of Xerox who benchmarked us on the same topic; they submitted only 11 questions to be covered during an eight-hour session. This more relaxed approach allowed sufficient time for follow-up questions and dialogue. The distinction between these two incidents is a combination of both benchmarking experience and the ability to follow a standard process. The value of following a process when conducting a benchmarking study is that the resulting information has a higher quality and is targeted more to your company's specific needs.

Figure 5 displays the simple model for benchmarking used in this workbook. This model parallels the plan-do-check-act sequence, applying a six-step process for understanding and implementing process change.[10]

The six steps in this model form the outline for Chapters 2 through 7 in this workbook. A case study and related discussion exercise are worked into the text at each step of the methodology to help you understand its application. Chapter 1 provides an introduction to process benchmarking, and Chapter 8 provides some ideas for integrating benchmarking into your planning process so that you can use benchmarking more effectively as a tool for continuous business improvement.

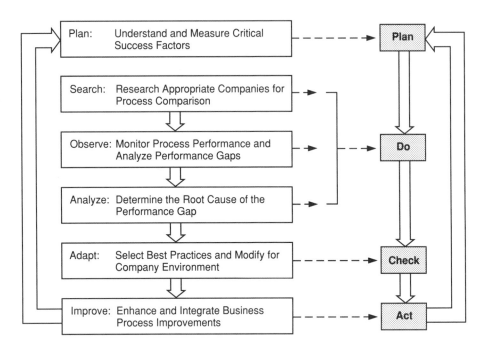

Figure 5. Process Benchmarking Model

Benchmarking is recognized by the board of examiners for the Malcolm Baldrige National Quality Award as a key quality tool for business process improvement.[11] This methodology is considered so important to enabling the success of TQM that benchmarking and competitive analysis were cited in 12 of the 32 evaluation criteria for the 1991 award. The question for most companies is no longer whether they should conduct benchmarking studies, but how they should conduct them. The purpose of this workbook is to guide you as you begin your benchmarking efforts.

NOTES

1. Gregory H. Watson, *Benchmarking for Competitive Advantage* (working title) (Cambridge, Mass.: Productivity Press, forthcoming).

2. Lawrence M. Miller, *Design for Total Quality: A Workbook for Socio-Technical Design* (Atlanta: The Miller Consulting Group, 1991), 23. This book is an excellent introduction to principles of organizational development used to facilitate the introduction of total quality management. Many of the principles that form the foundation for this work were introduced in the author's earlier work, *American Spirit: Visions of a New Corporate Culture* (New York: William Morrow, 1984).

3. Miller, *American Spirit* 137.

4. Robert C. Camp, *Benchmarking: The Search for Industry Best Practices That Lead to Superior Performance* (Milwaukee: Quality Press/Quality Resources, 1989), xi.

5. *Hoshin Kanri*, Yoji Akao, ed. (Cambridge, Mass.: Productivity Press, 1991).

6. Conformance quality is distinguished from perceived quality in Robert D. Buzzell and Bradley T. Gale's *The PIMS (Profit Impact of Market Strategy) Principles: Linking Strategy to Performance* (New York: Free Press, 1987), see Chap. 6.

7. Leonard M. Fuld, *Competitor Intelligence: How to Get It, How to Use It* (New York: John Wiley, 1985). The seminal work on competitive information management, this book is a particularly good reference to sources of secondary information to support benchmarking.

8. Michael Porter of Harvard Business School has written the most authoritative works on the market side of competitive analysis tools. His works include: *Competitive Strategy* (New York: Free Press, 1985) *Competitive Advantage* (New York: Free Press, 1985) *Competition in Global Industries* (Cambridge: Harvard University Press, 1986) and *Competitive Advantage of Nations* (New York: Free Press, 1990).

9. Kaiser Associates, Inc., *Beating the Competition: A Practical Guide to Benchmarking* (Vienna, Va: Kaiser Associates, Inc.,1988). This firm has produced two related publications: *Understanding the Competition: A Practical Guide to Competitive Analysis* and *Developing Industry Strategies: A Practical Guide to Industry Analysis*. Kaiser Associates is one of several consulting firms that specializes in conducting benchmarking studies.

10. I first proposed this six-step model in December 1989 to the benchmarking sub-committee of the GOAL/QPC research committee. GOAL/QPC has reported their research results as: "GOAL/QPC Research Report 91-01, Benchmarking" (Methuen, Mass., 1991).

11. Although benchmarking is a relatively recent quality tool, it has become widely accepted. It was specifically called out in the 1991 Malcolm Baldrige National Quality Award criteria for business process improvement and is used as a key measurement basis for both goal setting and evaluating results. The evaluation criteria call out benchmarking or competitive analysis in 12 of the 32 evaluation criteria sections. The pervasive use of this tool for TQM surpasses all other quality tools mentioned in the award criteria. The following are the Baldrige criteria sections that refer to benchmarking or competitive analysis as a recommended approach, deployment method, or tool for evaluating the results of the quality plan:

    1. Section 2.2 Competitive Comparisons and Benchmarks
    2. Section 3.1 Strategic Quality Planning Process
    3. Section 3.2 Quality Goals and Plans
    4. Section 4.4 Employee Recognition and Performance Measurement
    5. Section 4.5 Employee Well-being and Morale
    6. Section 6.1 Quality of Products and Services
    7. Section 6.2 Business Process and Support Services Quality Results
    8. Section 6.3 Supplier Quality Results
    9. Section 7.3 Customer Service Standards
    10. Section 7.4 Commitment to Customers
    11. Section 7.6 Customer Satisfaction Determination
    12. Section 7.7 Customer Satisfaction Results

1
Introducing Process Benchmarking

Core Competencies
Key Business Processes
Critical Success Factors
Conducting a Benchmarking Study
TQM and Benchmarking
Case Study

Just as water retains no constant shape, so in warfare there are no constant conditions.

— Sun Tzu

Process benchmarking is a continuous improvement tool for increasing the competitive performance of your company in its key business processes. The objective of a process benchmarking study is to improve a particular process. Process benchmarking usually begins with some indication that a particular process is performing inadequately. Such an indication may come from a customer complaint, management observation, or an employee suggestion. In any case, the observation is made relative to some standard of performance.

During the initial phase of benchmarking, the team uses the principles of data-driven decision making (management by fact) to establish the need for change. The benchmark or indicator for process performance measurement becomes the improvement standard. Setting the benchmark for a process is not an easy task; before a process is first benchmarked, there may have been no external standard for comparison.

Benchmarking is a commitment to continuous evaluation of business process performance. A benchmark cannot be ignored and allowed to stagnate as an historical anomaly. Rather, a benchmark is like Sun Tzu's water that "retains no constant shape." Competitive market forces tend to drive benchmark performance trends to ever-higher levels of attainment. A benchmark performance does not remain the standard for long.

CORE COMPETENCIES

It is important to use benchmarking as a tool for evaluating corporate strategy. In the search for those competitive advantages that are inherently sustainable, it is necessary to increase the rate of gaining "corporate knowledge" in the areas that represent *core competencies* for the business.[1] The functional consistency of a business comes from using a goal-oriented planning process to drive performance beyond the levels of competitors in the company's few critical success areas. Thus, benchmarking — gaining the knowledge of your company's relative position in key business processes and core competencies — is an essential aspect of the strategic planning process.

Because benchmarking requires continual analysis and reassessment, a company may have to concentrate its resources on monitoring only those benchmarks that indicate performance in core business competencies or those areas that distinguish the company's performance from that of its competitors.[2] The set of core competencies for a business may change over time as the business changes its strategic intentions. Each core competence must be reviewed to determine if it is still aligned with the strategic business intent. Core competence is defined as a capability that meets three tests:

1. It has a wide application in the company's business.
2. It should make a significant contribution to perceived customer benefits.
3. It should be difficult for a competitor to imitate.[3]

These core competencies can be found across all key business processes. Few companies will develop more than five or six areas of core competence under this definition, due to implicit restraints on their resources.[4] To clarify the application of the term, consider the following set of core competencies that was defined for one *Fortune* 50 business: customer service, technology transition from lab to product, time-to-market for new products, and product reliability improvement.

KEY BUSINESS PROCESSES

Since resources are limited for the more extensive benchmarking investigations, it is important to have the management team agree on which processes should receive this degree of analytical attention.[5] While all processes contribute to the functioning of a business, some are more critical to the business operation. These *key business processes* represent core functional efforts and are usually characterized by transactions that directly or indirectly influence the external customer's perception of the company. Key business processes tend to be cross-functional and require many of the company's resources for execution.

One way to determine a company's key business processes is to analyze its major business systems.[6] Figure 6 depicts a key business process matrix that can be used to determine those business processes that have the strongest influence across the business system. Across the top of the matrix are eight principal business systems, which are described as follows:

- *Control business* exercises strategic direction, financial control, and business planning.

- *Design products* seeks to understand customer requirements and expectations, translate them into product features, and design the product to deliver those features.[7]
- *Market products* promotes product sales and develop product descriptions, product pricing, and product packaging and documentation. In this model the system also includes sales-related processes.
- *Purchase materials* procures materials for manufacturing.
- *Produce products* transforms materials into assembled and tested products.
- *Distribute products* delivers products to the customer.
- *Service products* provides for product installation, repair, and upgrade.
- *Support business* manages the business infrastructure including facilities, mail, cafeteria, travel, transportation, etc.

By evaluating the strength of the relationships among the business processes in the left column of the matrix and their influence on each business system along the top row, you can determine the processes that have the most companywide influence. Using the appropriate icons (listed at the bottom of the matrix), grade the interaction between each process and system according to level of strength. Those processes that are candidates for key business processes should be the "critical few" that have the most influence across the entire business system. For instance, IBM has identified only 16, despite the size of its business; one of these is new product development.

Once you have identified the key business processes you can look at the core competencies that are found within these processes. While these key business processes are strong candidates for benchmarking studies, the core competencies should be required candidates for performance benchmarking and ongoing research.

CRITICAL SUCCESS FACTORS

"Critical success factors are the limited number of areas in which results, if they are satisfactory, will ensure successful competitive performance for the organization. They are the few key areas where 'things must go right' for the business to flourish. If results are not adequate, the organization's efforts for the period will be less than desired."[8] Clearly, a company's critical success factors should be linked to its core competencies and key business processes. In this workbook, critical success factors are defined as those quantifiable, measurable, and auditable indicators of process performance in a key business process.

Business Processes	Business Systems							
	Control Business	Design Products	Market Products	Purchase Materials	Produce Products	Distribute Products	Service Products	Support Business
Evaluate market information								
Develop business strategy								
Develop product requirements								
Conduct customer focus groups								
Develop customer relationships								
Perform customer surveys								
Analyze competitor performance								
Price products								
Forecast product sales								
Build prototype products								
Develop supplier relationship								
Procure and support capital equipment								
Document product design								
Plan production								
Manage incoming materials								
Assemble products								
Manage inventory								
Conduct final product test								
Package and store products								
Ship product								
Resolve customer complaints								
Perform field service								
Repair field returns								
Manage cash flow								
Evaluate and report performance								
Recruit employees								
Develop employees								
Manage and support facilities								

Relationship Strength: Strong △   Moderate ●   Weak ○

Figure 6. Key Business Process Matrix

Critical success factors are measured in basic business terms and are selected as measures of business effectiveness (quality), efficiency (cycle time), or economy (cost). These factors are also the basic process measures of TQM. Carefully selecting those measures that will be used for critical success factors is important to ensure that the study can be used for cross-company comparisons.[9] These measures tend to persist in the management system of a company. For instance, in 1987 Chief Executive John Young introduced a new critical success factor at Hewlett-Packard: breakeven time (BET). The BET metric was integrated into HP's new product development process over the next four years. Figure 7 is a worksheet for evaluating potential critical success factors to determine their effectiveness as benchmarks.

Since we have introduced core competencies, key business processes, and critical success factors, it will be helpful to reiterate their roles in benchmarking:

1. Core competencies describe strategic business capabilities that provide a company with a marketplace advantage. For instance, a core competence may be the ability to rapidly make the transition from prototype technology to production-ready status or the development of a distribution network to deliver products to customers.

2. Key business processes are those processes that influence the customer's perception of your business. Potential key business processes include new product development, where the price of a product is set and reliability levels determined; supplier management, where the underlying quality of the product is established; production or final assembly, where the delivered quality of the product is assured; and customer service and sales, where there is direct contact with the customer for delivery preference, installation effectiveness, and other support functions.

3. Critical success factors are the quantitative measures for effectiveness, economy, and efficiency; examples include time-to-market, product reliability (mean time between failures), supplier quality yield (sometimes called six sigma), first pass production yield, and production cycle time.

Although core competencies and key business processes help you understand your particular business environment and focus on benchmarking efforts, the critical success factors are used for the measure of comparison in a benchmarking study.

Key Business Process: _____

Proposed Critical Success Factor:_____

Reason Proposed: _____

_____

CSF Process Owner: _____

_____

Analysis for CSF Qualification

1. Is the proposed CSF quantifiable? _____ How? _____

_____

2. Is the proposed CSF measurable?_____ How? _____

_____

3. Is the proposed CSF auditable?_____ Where?_____

_____

4. Does the proposed CSF indicate process results over time? _____
   How? _____

_____

5. Does the proposed CSF indicate progress toward goal over time? _____
   How?_____

_____

6. How does a change in the key business process correlate with changes in the magnitude of the proposed
   CSF?_____

_____

_____

7. Is this measure for a proposed CSF accepted within your company? _____

_____

8. Is this proposed CSF measure widely accepted by other companies? _____
   Which companies? _____

_____

9. Is it easy to obtain data?_____ Is the data integrity reliable?_____
   Is the resulting CSF measure easily calculated?_____

_____

10. Is this proposed CSF reported in open literature? _____
    Where?_____

Figure 7. Critical Success Factor Worksheet

CONDUCTING A BENCHMARKING STUDY

To conduct a benchmarking study is to perform a research project. After establishing a quantitative performance level as a benchmark for a key business process, the management team uses objective assessment to qualify the practices that result in the quantitative performance. Industry surveys, process roundtables, and on-site visits are used to understand how these practices have been implemented.

C. William Emory defines research as a "systematic inquiry aimed at providing information to solve problems" and presents a list of seven characteristics of good research:

- The purpose of the research should be clearly defined.
- The research method should be repeatable.
- The research should be planned to provide objective results.
- The researchers should report any flaws in their research process and estimate the effect these may have on the results.
- The analysis should identify the significance of the results, and the methods used should be appropriate.
- Conclusions should be justified by the data.
- Greater confidence in a study occurs if the researcher is known and has a reputation for integrity.[10]

Benchmarking involves a systematic investigation of the targeted process. When benchmarking was initially publicized, it was likened to "industrial spying." Therefore, a high code of ethics is necessary in conducting benchmark studies. By protocol, most companies follow the practice of Xerox and ask that proprietary or confidential information not be divulged to them. Emory lists some questionable research practices that may also apply to benchmarking studies:

- Involving people in research without their knowledge or consent.
- Coercing people to participate.
- Withholding from the research participant the true nature of the research.
- Deceiving the research participant.
- Invading the privacy of the research participant.
- Failing to treat research participants fairly and to show them consideration and respect. [11]

Company values form the foundation of TQM. Many companies that practice TQM believe in values such as open communication, trust and trustworthiness, mutual respect, teamwork, consensus, and participation in decision making. By practicing TQM, a company moves in the right direction to participate in the ethical practice of benchmarking.

TQM AND BENCHMARKING

A planned approach to benchmarking is necessary to gain the full value of your time investment. The discussion of process benchmarking is structured using the six-step model presented in the introduction: plan, search, observe, analyze, adapt, and improve. The goal of the benchmarking project is to continuously improve a key business process with the objective of achieving customer satisfaction that exceeds the satisfaction delivered by your competitors. (As a note to any reader who believes this may not be an appropriate objective for a process that has internal customers: I believe that every process has a virtual competitor. For instance, if your process is developing graphics for a document, then your competitors are external graphics companies or perhaps the clip art software packages. Almost any process could be considered for subcontracting to another source. Therefore, beware of your virtual competitor!)

So, what does it take to do a benchmarking study? Figure 8 contains a checklist that follows the six-step benchmarking process. We will use it to guide our progress as we study benchmarking.

A case study about a hypothetical company, Martin Industries, is used to provide insights into the benchmarking process. Each chapter provides a description of a Martin Industries benchmarking project, followed by a brief exercise with questions for you to answer. This case study is designed to get you thinking about your benchmarking requirements and to provide a starting point for your first study.

Plan	☐ What is our process?
	☐ How does our process work?
	☐ How do we measure it?
	☐ How well is our process performing today?
	☐ Who are our customers?
	☐ What products and services do we deliver to our customers?
	☐ What do our customers expect or require of our products and services?
	☐ What is our performance goal?
	☐ How did we establish that goal?
	☐ How does our products and service performance compare with our competitors?
Search	☐ What companies perform this process better?
	☐ Which company is the best at performing this process?
	☐ What can we learn from that company?
	☐ Whom should we contact to determine if they are willing to participate in our study?
Observe	☐ What is their process?
	☐ What is their performance goal?
	☐ How well does their process perform over time and at multiple locations?
	☐ How do they measure process performance?
	☐ What enables the performance of their process?
	☐ What factors could inhibit the adaptation of their process into our company?
Analyze	☐ What is the nature of the performance gap?
	☐ What is the magnitude of the performance gap?
	☐ What characteristics distinguish their process as superior?
	☐ What activities within our process are candidates for change?
Adapt	☐ How does the knowledge of their process enable us to improve our process?
	☐ Should we redefine our performance measure or reset our performance goal based upon this benchmark?
	☐ What activities within their process would need to be modified to adapt it into our business environment?
Improve	☐ What have we learned during this benchmarking study that will allow us to improve upon the "superior" process?
	☐ How can we implement these changes into our process?

Figure 8. Benchmarking Study Checklist

CASE STUDY

Why benchmark? For the management of Martin Industries, it was a pragmatic issue: they were losing market share to two competitors and needed to regain their competitive position.

Martin Industries produces mechanical adding machines, and, until four years ago, they had dominated this industry with 100 percent of the market share.[12] In its annual report of only three years ago, Martin noted that personal computers were an interesting adjunct to the market.[13] In that year, personal computers gained 10 percent market share of the mechanical adding machine market. The following year, Martin's annual report noted that personal computers were increasing their foothold, but that the market remained firmly in the hands of the mechanical adding machines. Martin's market share was then down to 82 percent.

Last year, Martin noted that it had recently commenced a development project for a personal computer that was dedicated to the cash register function. Martin has been able to field a standard mechanical adding machine product to market in an average of three and a half years. However, the company had little experience in electronics design and manufacture; it sank 8.9 percent of sales revenue into this project, code-named Valiant. The company's market share faced additional erosion as IBM and Compaq personal computers cut further into the market and garnered a full 42 percent share. Martin was forced to take cost-cutting measures, reducing the work force by 38 percent and cutting the wages of the remaining employees by 10 percent across the board.

The members of the Valiant Project Team were faced with a significant development problem. They believed their specialized electronic adding machine could be produced at lower cost than the generic personal computer it was pitted against; however, they also believed that their competition held some manufacturing advantages over them. The team members were not sure where they stood relative to the competition but decided they must try to understand. Hence, Martin's interest in benchmarking.

The remaining market research professional at Martin had read about benchmarking and suggested they merge benchmarking with their customer satisfaction survey to discover where they had room to improve over their targeted competitors. From their study of benchmarking, they realized they should not restrict themselves to their own industry but should learn from other industries that had faced similar problems. The idea struck them that the

American automotive industry dealt with similar problems and that Ford had faced a similar challenge when they conceived of Team Taurus.[14] Perhaps this would give them a good model for their problem. They also recognized that Xerox had dealt with a similar problem when Canon, Ricoh, and other Japanese copier manufacturers assaulted the photocopier market in the early 1980s.[15] Kodak was a third example of a company whose camera product line was besieged by the Japanese, yet they too managed to improve their degree of competitiveness. Thus, the Valiant Team defined their benchmarking project. Join us in the next few chapters as we trace the progress of their Valiant effort.

Exercise

Using the benchmarking study checklist form in Figure 8, trace the progress of the Valiant Team as they continue their study. Consider whether they missed any elements of the benchmarking process that would provide them with significant value. What would you do differently from the Valiant Team? Has Martin's management team established the foundation for a successful project? Look also at the key business process matrix (Figure 6). How could this matrix help Martin identify the appropriate processes for its benchmarking study? How should the Valiant Team use the CSF (critical success factor) worksheet?

NOTES

1. This term originated in Gary Hamel and C.K. Prahalad, "Strategic Intent," *Harvard Business Review* (May-June 1989) 65. The authors note that few Western companies have a good track record in anticipating the moves of their global competitors. They believe that the problem is in the way that companies approach competitive analysis. Typically, an analysis consists of looking at the existing resources of current competitors rather than at those who have resourcefulness and a capability to rapidly build competitive differentiation. Companies that have become recognized industry leaders over the past 20 years invariably had ambitions that surpassed their resources and capabilities, but they were not bound by those facts. They pursued an obsession that Hamel and Prahalad call "strategic intent." They cite examples of Komatsu who sought to "Encircle Caterpillar," and Canon, whose motto was "Beat Xerox."

2. The Motorola benchmarking course material describes distinctive competencies: "Those unique competencies which provide a clear and long-term sustainable competitive advantage in the market place and are demonstrably different in the eyes of the customer."

3. James C. Abegglen and George Stalk, Jr. *Kaisha: The Japanese Corporation* (New York: Basic Books, 1985). The authors report that the model followed for competitive advantage by Japanese companies is based on benchmarking as a key ingredient: "Be better. If you can't be better, be different."

4. C.K. Prahalad and Gary Hamel, "The Core Competence of the Corporation," *Harvard Business Review* (May-June 1990): 83-84. The authors have suggested that core competencies refer to those technical capabilities that "spawn unanticipated products." Their focus is on the technical capabilities of a company such as integrated circuit design. I am suggesting a broader usage to include any key process that meets an expanded application beyond the technical product areas. I am using core competencies to refer to any aspect of the business operation that results in a strategic market advantage. This would include customer service and product distribution as well as product development.

5. Again, quoting from the Motorola benchmarking course material: "Benchmarking requires hunting for data that is often difficult to find. It is usually gathered in bits and pieces and then assembled to reveal a pattern. To minimize the research effort, a planned data collection approach that finds

sources quickly and avoids duplication of effort should be followed. In any event, plan to spend considerable time collecting data in the public domain."

6. The following hierarchy is used in discussing a business structure: systems are composed of processes; processes are composed of activities; activities are composed of tasks; and tasks are composed of steps. Benchmarking looks within processes at the conduct of activities.

7. The word "product" in this book refers to either a product or a service.

8. John F. Rockart's "Chief Executives Define Their Own Data Needs," *Harvard Business Review* (March-April, 1979). Using Rockart's definition of critical factors, examples of potential critical success factors include productivity, technology, customer relations, research and development, new product introduction, overhead cost structure, and facilities. In this book, I use a tighter definition to imply the process performance measures that indicate the quantitative level of performance for a key business process. For instance, for research and development, the critical success factor would be time-to-market for a new product.

9. Several books on measurement of productivity, cost, quality, and cycle time are helpful. Three of the most helpful include Richard S. Sloma, *How to Measure Managerial Performance* (New York: Macmillan Co., 1980) which presents a smorgasbord of management measures for all significant managerial processes; William F. Christopher, *Productivity Measurement Handbook*, 2nd ed. (Cambridge, Mass.: Productivity Press, 1985) which presents tools for measuring productivity in almost any kind of work environment; C. William Emory, *Business Research Methods*, 3rd ed. (Homewood, Ill.: Dow Jones-Irwin, 1985) which presents a sound methodology for approaching research in business. Other books that may provide assistance include Robert S. Kaplan, *Measures for Manufacturing Excellence* (Boston: Harvard Business School Press, 1990); Carol J. McNair, William Mosconi, and Thomas F. Norris, *Beyond the Bottom Line: Measuring World Class Performance* (Homewood, Ill: Dow Jones-Irwin, 1989), and Will Kaydos, *Measuring, Managing, and Maximizing Performance* (Cambridge, Mass.: Productivity Press, 1991).

10. Emory, *Business Research*, 10-12.

11. Emory, *Business Research*, 12.

12. This case study is adapted from the story of National Cash Register, told in Richard Foster, *Innovation: The Attacker's Advantage* (New York: Summit Books, 1986). The actual situation of NCR has been modified by projecting to the current business environment. The information presented about Ford,

Hewlett-Packard, IBM, Intel, Kodak, and Xerox is available to the avid benchmarker through secondary source investigation. The case is a realistic example of a benchmarking project conducted by a first-time benchmarker.

13. A survey of successes and failures in the computer industry that should not be missed is in Danny Miller, *The Icarus Paradox* (New York: Harper Business, 1990). Case studies discussed in Miller's book include Apple Computer, Control Data Corporation, Digital Equipment Corporation, IBM, Sun Microsystems, Texas Instruments, and Wang Laboratories. Clyde V. Prestowitz, Jr., *Trading Places* (New York: Basic Books, 1988), describes the transformation of the semiconductor industry from a position of American leadership to Japanese leadership. This book could have provided additional comparisons for the Valiant Team and may have led to recommending Motorola Corporation as another target company for their benchmarking study.

14. James P. Womack, Daniel T. Jones, and Daniel Roos, *The Machine That Changed the World* (New York: Rawson Associates, 1990). This book reports on the results of a five-year MIT study of the automobile industry. This study provides an excellent background for benchmarking any automotive firm.

15. The story of the Xerox rebound from the Japanese assault on its copier market is described in Gary Jacobson and John Hillkirk, *Xerox: American Samurai* (New York: Macmillan Co., 1986). The authors introduce the term *dantotsu*, translated from the Japanese means "striving to be the best of the best." This book is excellent historical reading about the early application of benchmarking by Xerox to turn around its market share loss.

2
Planning a Benchmarking Study

Deciding What to Benchmark
Determining Customer Needs
Understanding the Business Model
Profiling the Process
Developing the Benchmarking Plan
Case Study

Step by step walk the thousand-mile road.
                                                    — Miyamoto Musashi

DECIDING WHAT TO BENCHMARK

Xerox positions benchmarking as a continuous learning experience that supports ongoing process improvement; it uses benchmarking as a way to define and control change to ensure that changes have positive results.[1] Tom Carter, vice president of quality at Alcoa, says: "We benchmark for a purpose: to add value."[2] Benchmarking provides an insider's view of another company's operation in a way that identifies distinctions between the practices of the two companies.[3]

The first step in benchmarking is to plan the study. This plan should fit within the mosaic of the companywide quality plan, which, in turn, should be integrated with the strategic business plan.[4] This strong linkage to the quality planning process and strategic business plan is evidence of process benchmarking's support of TQM. Each benchmarking study is a journey along Musashi's "thousand-mile road" and requires many steps.

To plan the benchmarking study, you need to understand your company's business environment. This helps you identify your key business processes and where you have problems today; it also helps you develop the parameters that define your choice of what processes to benchmark. Benchmarking measures not only what is produced (in terms of products and services) but also how it is produced. Benchmarking should complement the establishment of measurement systems that monitor your business's critical success factors. Business measurement is a prerequisite to benchmarking.

Before we discuss the benchmarking plan for a specific study project, we should cover the preliminaries that permit the integration of benchmarking into the strategic business planning process. These considerations include senior management commitment, the business environment, customer and market segmentation, and the business enterprise model. Once these factors are understood, you have defined the context for process benchmarking.

Deciding what to benchmark begins with the commitment of senior management to dedicate the resources necessary for benchmarking. This commitment should be an open statement of their support for a degree of benchmarking around particular topics that are determined to be relevant to the business. If benchmarking is only a grass-roots-level effort, the team may not be able to gain admittance to the world-class corporations it needs. Quality directors at such companies selectively decide whether to invest their time and resources in a proposed study. Senior management commitment and support is necessary to gain access to world-class processes.

The decision to implement benchmarking should be accompanied by an analysis of the business environment. This analysis defines the broad direction of the benchmarking studies. A business environment analysis follows the model suggested in the introduction (see Figure 1). Figure 9 presents an approach for analyzing the environment of your business.

The factors suggested in this model provide an external view of your business. Most of this information is reviewed on a regular basis by a senior management team. There are five areas that need to be considered: competitors as a function of market share; regulatory agencies concerned with safety, environmental, health, customs, quality, and administrative regulations; major accounts categorized by their major industry (standard industry classification numbers are a reasonable first cut); critical suppliers who provide strategic technologies for your products or services; and the major economic indicators, values, and trends that predict your industry performance.

Once the business environment has been defined, this information may be correlated with the key business process and critical success factor analyses developed in the first chapter. This aligns the internal view of your company with an external perspective. Those key business processes affected by the current environmental situation are your primary candidates for benchmarking.

After identifying these processes, establish process ownership—who is responsible for the performance and continuous improvement of that process. Process owners need to sponsor and participate in the proposed benchmarking study. These owners need to validate the relevance of the study and, by applying the principles of TQM, determine the significance of this proposed study to their customers. The next step in determining what specifically to benchmark is to better understand the perspective of your customers.

DETERMINING CUSTOMER NEEDS

The process for benchmarking has been expressed in a variety of ways, beginning with the Xerox model[5] and continuing on to a variety of other models.[6] Many of these processes share the need to understand the perspective of

Competitors:

Name   Market Share

1. _____   _____
2. _____   _____
3. _____   _____
4. _____   _____
5. _____   _____
6. _____   _____
7. _____   _____

Regulatory Agencies:

Name   Type

1. _____   _____
2. _____   _____
3. _____   _____
4. _____   _____
5. _____   _____
6. _____   _____
7. _____   _____

Major Accounts:

Name   Industry

1. _____   _____
2. _____   _____
3. _____   _____
4. _____   _____
5. _____   _____
6. _____   _____
7. _____   _____

Critical Suppliers:

Name   Technology

1. _____   _____
2. _____   _____
3. _____   _____
4. _____   _____
5. _____   _____
6. _____   _____
7. _____   _____

Economic Indicator:

Name   Value   Trend

1. _____   _____   _____
2. _____   _____   _____
3. _____   _____   _____
4. _____   _____   _____
5. _____   _____   _____
6. _____   _____   _____
7. _____   _____   _____

Figure 9. Business Environment Model

the internal or external customer of the benchmarked process — the expression of the customer's needs, requirements, expectations, or complaints. But the question remains: What to benchmark? While Bob Camp suggests a list of questions based on your company's mission statement, goals, objectives, customer concerns, product issues, and competitive pressures, we will focus on the basic TQM principle — viewing the benchmarked process from the customer's perspective.[7]

The fundamental business-process model tracks the material and information flow of a business:

$$\text{supplier} \rightarrow \text{input} \rightarrow \text{process} \rightarrow \text{output} \rightarrow \text{customer}$$

The principal objective of the planning step is to understand and measure processes for critical success factors from the customer's perspective.

Who is the customer of the process? It depends on the process. Your company's external customers are not always the consumers of your products. For instance, the customers of your company's financial results are stock-market analysts, business journalists, boards of directors, and most importantly the stockholders. Customers of your employee safety and health systems include the Occupational Safety and Health Administration, your local emergency service branches of government and hospitals and the local community residents around your facilities, as well as the families of your employees. You must be able to identify specifically your customers in order to evaluate their needs. It is also important to determine how the suppliers of your process influence the ultimate performance of your process in the eyes of its customers.

A first step in analyzing your customer's expectations is to evaluate your process output. The initial Xerox benchmarking efforts focused on competitive benchmarking, concentrating on competitive product, service, process, and practice performance. You can begin your understanding of the different segments of your company's external customers' expectations by developing a profile of their attributes. This customer-segmentation model focuses on your company's product and service output and gives an understanding of the consumption of these outputs by the ultimate customer. (If the market research group in your company has already completed a customer-segmentation model for your company, then this exercise need not be done again.)

Customer-segmentation modeling (see Figure 10) consists of three phases: analyzing the product profile, evaluating product applications, and profiling the customers who use that product. In the product profiling phase, the key product features are detailed and compared to customer requirements and expectations. A good quality tool used to perform this analysis is quality function deployment (QFD), which has been applied extensively in the automotive industry.[8] The second phase, evaluating product applications, considers the way groups or categories of customers in the market use that particular product and how that product relates to competing technologies and products. While QFD is useful for recording this information, product positioning analyses and reverse engineering can help sort the data. The third phase, profiling the customers, examines the individual consumers of the product by application. In many companies the sales organization will maintain this field-level information, which is supported by classic market tools of industry analysis and market segmentation.

After completing this analysis, you need to evaluate how the chosen benchmark process influences the customer's perceptions. Look for specific process outputs that are evident from the beginning of the sales process through the lifetime of the support and service processes. By identifying each of the key process's customer touch-points, you will be able to focus the benchmark study on improving the customer perception of your company and making a competitive difference. For instance, if product delivery is important to the customer, some of the affected processes would be order processing, product distribution, production planning, material purchasing, and production assembly processes. This customer-focused analysis provides background information for defining the scope and direction of the study. The next phase of the planning process is to identify how this study fits into the company's business model.

UNDERSTANDING THE BUSINESS MODEL

One final step is needed before you have finished putting your first benchmarking study into an appropriate business context. This step involves developing a model for the business enterprise as a whole. This model provides a planning framework for regular analysis of strategic (breakthrough) business objectives and tactical (basic process or fundamental business process) objectives. Both the business enterprise model and the business planning framework rely on a tool such as process benchmarking to support continuous process improvement.

Product Profile	Product Application	Customer Profile
Company Output	**Type of Application**	**Type of Company**
Key product features • quality • performance • safety • value-to-price Key service features • quality • performance • delivery • value-to-price	Market size Product features used Service features used Competing products Relationship factors • quality • value-to-price • service • delivery • safety Dissatisfaction factors • performance • features • quality • value-to-price • service • delivery • safety	Company size Industry (four-digit SIC) Geographic locations Product annual demand Percent product share Buying factors • features • performance • quality • safety • value-to-price • delivery • service Organization structure • decision maker • procurement officer • end user Product applications
Applicable Tool: Quality Function Deployment	**Applicable Tools:** Product Positioning Reverse Engineering	**Applicable Tools:** Industry Analysis Market Segmentation

Figure 10. Customer-Segmentation Model

The concept of the business enterprise model can be represented as a business system that integrates internal services with key business processes and the external market or product delivery system. An illustration of this concept of business enterprise modeling is presented in Figure 11.

It is important to evaluate your business from a market segmentation perspective and to identify customers and suppliers of key processes in terms of their information dialogues with your business about their requirements, expectations, perceptions, and complaints. One method that more fully describes the business environment model takes a systems approach by modeling all major business system interactions for information, material, control, and resource flows. An innovative approach to this modeling effort is an extension of a methodology developed by the U.S. Air Force to support their computer-integrated manufacturing technology project of the mid-1970s. Several major business organizations have adapted this methodology, called IDEF, to present a

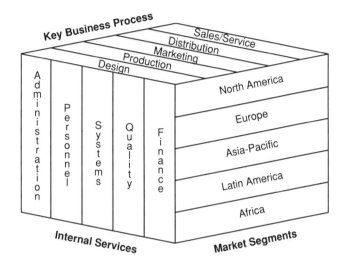

Figure 11. Business Enterprise Model

detailed perspective of the interactions among business systems. The output of this method not only can be used for improving business understanding and documenting process requirements, but it is also an excellent foundation for developing the management information structure of a corporation.[9]

Once the overall business environment, customer segmentation model, and enterprise model are understood, the particular process is in an appropriate context to perform a benchmarking study.

PROFILING THE PROCESS

Many benchmarkers consider self-learning and process profiling the first step in their study. This step in the planning phase of benchmarking is similar to doing your homework. It involves self-study of the proposed benchmark process and an examination of those factors that influence process performance. The objective of this study is to determine the most critical process parameters that influence performance. This step includes documenting your process and identifying the process output and the customers for that output; it concludes with the collecting and analyzing of process performance data. The level of process performance and trends in this information are used to establish an internal measurement baseline for comparison with the external processes. Figure 12 is a job aid for collecting the information gathered during this analysis.

Process Output: _____
_____
_____
_____
_____

Process Customer: _____
_____

Process Performance Measures:		Current Level	Trend
Quality	First-pass yield	_____	_____
	Customer returns	_____	_____
	Process completion/plan ratio	_____	_____
Cost	Process cost	_____	_____
	Process value-add	_____	_____
	Value-to-cost ratio	_____	_____
Cycle	Work-in-process inventory	_____	_____
Time	Process cycle time	_____	_____
	Process changeover time	_____	_____
	Process downtime	_____	_____

Process Performance Goals:	Short-term	Long-term
First pass yield	_____	_____
Value-to-cost ratio	_____	_____
Cycle time	_____	_____

Process Activity Diagram:

Figure 12. Process Performance Profile

While most of the information on this profile is straightforward, you need to provide definitions for your own process performance measures along with a short rationale for each specific metric. Most TQM programs consider the basic categories of process performance measurement to be quality, cost, and cycle time.

The three process performance goals proposed are first-pass yield, value-to-cost ratio, and cycle time. These goals reflect the fundamental TQM measures. First-pass yield is the measure of effectiveness for a process in performing its transaction for the first time without defects. Value-to-cost ratio is a measure of process economy in terms of its ability to produce higher value of output for lower levels of process cost. This is one measure of economy that is supported by activity-based cost-management methods. The third goal of cycle time reflects the "time is money" attitude of just-in-time manufacturing. Cycle time is a measure of process efficiency in terms of the amount of time consumed for each transaction. By focusing on improving all three measures, a process owner produces higher quality products, in less time, and for less cost. This is a fundamental objective of a generic business process.

The ten process performance measures provide detail that supports the measurement of the three goals. By first taking these measures, it becomes clearer how to set the goals. For instance, process cost and process value-add allow the calculation of the value-to-cost ratio. Work-in-process inventory, process cycle time, process changeover time, and process downtime all influence the analysis of the time efficiency of the process. First-pass yield, customer returns, and process completion-to-plan ratio all support the analysis of the quality for the transaction function of the process. (Please note that these measures are intended to be general; more process-specific measures may be used for any particular process.)

Before completing the planning process, a study team should establish performance measures and data collection methods for internal study. The team should also collect internal information and quantify the data and then analyze, simplify, and reformat the data into a performance record. Once these steps are completed, the team is ready to develop the benchmarking plan.

DEVELOPING THE BENCHMARKING PLAN

The plan itself is not a detailed document, but rather a flow of activities that you want to accomplish, accompanied by a set of guidelines for conducting the study. Some of the guidelines you need to establish include the following:

- The identity of the customer (champion or sponsor) of the study and the type of involvement or reporting relationship that they desire
- The urgency or schedule requirements for completing the study
- The scope of the results desired by project milestone dates
- A description of management's prejudices, biases, or preconceptions regarding the study: who is the best, what measures are traditional for this process, the goal performance that they believe is economical, the resource constraints that they apply to the process, etc.
- A recommendation of the team members to perform the study and a conscious commitment by management to permit them the time and budget to carry out the study

Consolidate this information into a formal plan and get the approval of both the process owner and the senior manager who is responsible for this business area. Select the team for the study and have the study sponsor or process owner notify the team members of their assignment. Provide an awareness presentation to the team that outlines the project, and gain their commitment to take training in the benchmarking process. Now you are prepared to begin the external research phase of benchmarking.

CASE STUDY

As a preliminary stage in their research, The Valiant Team prepared a Business Environment Model to give them a broad picture of their business from an external perspective (see Figure 13).

While Martin senior management had set some broad boundaries for the benchmarking project, they did not want to restrict the project team, so they asked them to attend a benchmarking course to start off their project on the right foot.[10] During the course they learned a simple six-step process for benchmarking and decided to follow it. For the plan step, they needed to define their project by determining the critical success factors for their selected key business process and measuring their performance in these areas. This step requires that they identify and understand their process. The Valiant Team decided to benchmark the product delivery process (PDP) by which their products reach the customer. This process defines, designs, develops, and delivers products for their market; it includes the relationships between research and development (R&D), marketing, and manufacturing operations. The Valiant Team took three weeks to understand and measure this process. They discovered that the customers of their PDP included sales and service as well as their products' end users.

The key measure that Martin used for this process had been design-to-cost, producing a product at a fixed production cost and developing it under a fixed product design budget. The team discovered that the company wasn't particularly good in its performance in this area. Product development costs overran their initial estimated budgets by an average of 22 percent, and they exceeded their design-to-cost goals for the product only by an average of 8 percent. The team questioned why the goals had been established. One discovery the team made during their background research was that McKinsey & Company (a management consulting firm) had done a study of the time-to-market impact of cost and schedule trade-offs on the lifetime profitability of development projects.[11] The study indicated that delivery of products on schedule was by far a more important influence on product profitability than delivery on budget. In fact, budgets could be exceeded by as much as 50 percent before the effect would equal the market effect of a six-month delay in product introduction. The Valiant Team decided that cost goals were the wrong measure to look at and turned instead to time-based measures.

During their literature search on time-to-market information, the team discovered that a product of similar complexity — a new-generation printer —

Competitors:

	Name	Market Share
1.	MARTIN	58%
2.	COMPETITORS - SEVERAL	42%
3.		
4.		
5.		
6.		
7.		

Regulatory Agencies:

	Name	Type
1.	FCC	COMMUNICATIONS
2.	OSHA	SAFETY
3.	UL	SAFETY
4.	STATE TAX DEPARTMENTS	SALES TAX
5.		
6.		
7.		

Major Accounts:

	Name	Industry
1.	XEROX	ELECTRONICS
2.	HEWLETT-PACKARD	ELECTRONICS
3.	FRITO-LAY	FOOD
4.	PROCTER + GAMBLE	CONSUMER
5.	FEDERATED DEPARTMENT STORES	RETAIL SALES
6.		
7.		

Critical Suppliers:

	Name	Technology
1.	HEWLETT-PACKARD	CHIPS
2.	INTEL	CHIPS
3.	ZYLON	PCA'S
4.	MOTOROLA	CHIPS
5.	MEMORY	CHIPS
6.	AMP	CABLE
7.	HITACHI	DISPLAY

Economic Indicators:

	Name	Value	Trend
1.	COST OF LIVING INDEX	4%	UP
2.			
3.			
4.			
5.			
6.			
7.			

Figure 13. Business Environment Model

was developed in only 22 months by Hewlett-Packard, down from about four years for the previous generation printer. This was the kind of performance improvement that the Valiant Team wanted to achieve. After a survey of industry analysts, their market research professional estimated that their competitors were able to deliver significant product model changes in less than 12 months of engineering effort.

Exercise

Evaluate the business environment model developed by the Valiant Team. In what areas should they seek additional information or clarify the information they have obtained?

Based on the information presented, how would you structure the search phase of your process? Look at the critical success factor worksheet (Figure 7). How could the Martin team have improved their approach to process measurement? How could the business environment model (Figure 9) have helped them during this project phase? Review the customer segmentation model and the business enterprise model (Figures 10 and 11). How could the Valiant Team use these tools to clarify their project at this early phase? What information is needed to complete the process performance profile for their PDP (Figure 12)?

NOTES

1. A good description of Xerox Corporation's approach to benchmarking is found in their 1989 reference guide: Xerox Corporate Education and Training, "Benchmarking for Quality Improvement" (Stamford, Conn., document number 700P06130). This publication summarizes the material introduced in Bob Camp's *Benchmarking* book.

2. A recent discussion of the AT&T and Alcoa benchmarking processes is presented by Karen Bemowski, "The Benchmarking Bandwagon," *Quality Progress* (January 1991): 21.

3. Perhaps one of the best analogies of the application of benchmarking in business: Steven Walleck, "A Business View of World-Class Performers," *Wall Street Journal* (August 26, 1991). The author, who is director of McKinsey & Company's Cleveland office, stated: "Benchmarking . . . is a way to go backstage and watch another company's performance from the wings, where all the stage tricks and hurried realignments are visible. If the performance you choose to benchmark is world class, you will learn a lot about the art of management from this inside angle." Benchmarking, compared with competitive analysis, provides a deep understanding of the processes and skills that create superior performance.

4. Gregory H. Watson, *Managing for Consensus* (Cambridge, Mass.: Productivity Press, forthcoming), another book in this Productivity Press TQM set, describes more fully the nature of the quality planning process and its integration with the strategic business planning process and on implementing *hoshin kanri*. This book provides more detail on implementing *hoshin kanri* planning than Dr. Yoji Akao's book cited in the notes to the introduction.

5. Xerox Corporation, *Competitive Benchmarking: What It Is and What It Can Do for You* (Stamford, Conn., 1987). This updated version of the earlier "Red Book" on benchmarking is an internal summary of the Xerox benchmarking process (no document number).

6. A number of articles about benchmarking have appeared, beginning in 1984, that provide valuable insights into the development of this practice. William F. Galvin, "Competitive Benchmarking: A Technique Utilized by Xerox to Revitalize Itself to a Modern Competitive Position," *Review of Business*, (Winter, 1984): 6. Timothy R. Furey, "Benchmarking: The Key to Developing Competitive Advantage in Mature Markets," *Planning Review* (Sept.-Oct. 1987): 15. Frances Gaither Tucker, Seymour M. Zivan, and Robert C. Camp,

"How to Measure Yourself Against the Best," *Harvard Business Review* (Jan.-Feb. 1987). Carol Kennedy, "Xerox Charts a New Strategic Direction," *Long Range Planning* (Feb. 1989): 22. Robert M. Fifer, "Cost Benchmarking Functions on the Value Chain," *Planning Review* (May-June 1989). Lawrence S. Pryor, "Benchmarking: A Self-Improvement Strategy," *The Journal of Business Strategy*, (Nov.-Dec. 1989). Richard J. Maturi, "Benchmarking: The Search for Quality," *The Financial Manager* (March-April 1990). H. James Harrington, "Benchmarking" (Los Gatos, Calif.: Aug. 1990), (TR90.009HJH). The author is Ernst & Young's international quality advisor.

7. Camp, *Benchmarking*, 41-44.

8. QFD is a method for ensuring quality throughout each step of the product development process. QFD was first introduced in Japan by Dr. Yoji Akao in 1966 and first deployed in a full design system at Mitsubishi's Kobe Shipyards in the mid-1970s. Two firms specialize in teaching QFD methods: American Supplier Institute in Dearborn, Michigan (phone: [313] 336-8877) and GOAL/QPC in Methuen, Massachusetts (phone: [508] 685-3900). Books on QFD include William E. Eureka & Nancy E. Ryan, *The Customer-Driven Company: Managerial Perspectives in QFD* (Dearborn, Mich.: ASI Press, 1988), Yoji Akao, ed., *Quality Function Deployment: Integrating Customer Requirements into Product Design* (Cambridge, Mass.: Productivity Press, 1990), Bob King, *Better Designs in Half the Time*, 3rd ed., (Methuen, Mass.: GOAL/QPC Press, 1989).

9. A commercialized version of IDEF, the U.S. Air Force integrated computer-aided manufacturing (ICAM) definition language. David A. Marca and Clement L. McGowan, *Structured Analysis and Design Technique* (New York: McGraw-Hill, 1989) presents the IDEF methodology for documenting processes and establishing cross-functional process relationships is used by many of the larger computer companies, including IBM, Hewlett-Packard, and Digital Equipment. This methodology is one way to understand which processes are critical to the business function and are candidates for benchmarking. IDEF is superior to data flow diagraming techniques because it considers information, material, control, and resource flows rather than purely data flows. IDEF addresses processes from the viewpoint of the user or customer rather than the information specialist who is developing a piece of software. The commercial version of IDEF is called Structured Analysis and Design Technique (SADT)®, which is a registered trademark of Softech, Inc. Software for applying IDEF methods is available from a number of

sources including the DesignIDEF package from MetaSoftware in Cambridge, Mass. Gregory H. Watson, *Improving Your Process* (working title), the fourth book in this Productivity Press TQM set, presents IDEF as a method for the design of a companywide quality system.

10. The American Productivity and Quality Center (APQC) is a nonprofit organization dedicated to improving the quality and productivity of American industry. APQC is located in Houston, Texas, and information about membership and courses may be requested by calling (713) 681-4020. The Association for Manufacturing Excellence (AME), another nonprofit organization whose charter focuses on manufacturing process improvement, also conducts benchmarking seminars and may be contacted by calling (708) 520-3282.

11. The McKinsey & Company study is cited in Preston G. Smith and Donald G. Reinertsen, *Developing Products in Half the Time* (New York: Van Nostrand Reinhold, 1991).

3
Searching for World-Class Processes

Directing the Search
Leveraging Strategic Relationships
Using Secondary Sources
Summarizing Secondary Information
Selecting Best-in-Class Companies to Visit
Case Study

The principle of strategy is having one thing, to know ten thousand things.
— Miyamoto Musashi

DIRECTING THE SEARCH

The search phase of the benchmarking project is often the most difficult for a novice benchmarker. During this phase, the benchmark team needs to use the knowledge gained in their internal process study to determine which companies are most appropriate for external process comparisons. They must then perform open literature research on these companies, obtain permission for site visits, and develop the questionnaire that will guide the site visit. A primary objective of this benchmarking step is to translate the model and data requirements of your company's processes into a survey of industrywide best practices and performance measurements. This requires an understanding of secondary research tantamount to that of a legal research assistant or a doctoral student working on a dissertation. This chapter focuses on the two critical areas that support this research: a secondary data search and a method for identifying company performance that would warrant further investigation at a site-visit level.

The objective of this phase of the study is to compile the fragments of information found in a variety of sources so that a coherent picture of the business performance of the target benchmark companies can be formulated. During this step along the "thousand-mile road" we will be attempting to put together the picture of a company's operation using external sources — to "know many things" from the evidence collected.

LEVERAGING STRATEGIC RELATIONSHIPS

An important starting point for your research is to collect the information your organization already has about the targeted benchmark companies. This information comes from your investigation of your internal process documentation and market research that supports the processes used to understand the business environment, customer segmentation, and the process profile covered in Chapter 1.

One way to organize this information is to create a chart of relevant performance measurements and process steps for each of the companies (either competitors or world-class potentials) found in your earlier investigations.

Add companies to this list as your research uncovers new information that indicates companies with high performance. Then fill in each cell of the chart with the information you already have about the company; this helps identify gaps in your knowledge and understanding about a company's operations. You could even use the CEDAC method (cause and effect diagram with the addition of cards) to record information from your various internal sources.[1] By placing a CEDAC board in a benchmarking "war room," you present an opportunity for wide participation in capturing the current level of process knowledge and information and will be able to rapidly shape the research requirements of your study.

The next phase of the search is to take advantage of established strategic business alliances with companies that have a vested interest in your performance: suppliers, customers (particularly major accounts), trade associations and industry standards organizations, and companies that you have formed strategic alliances with regarding product requirements and marketing.[2] Attempting to match the business model of these companies with your company is important for understanding some of the different decision drivers behind their process and specifically identify where they have improved process performance beyond your company's current capability.

There is an ethical dimension to this phase of the study.[3] The use of suppliers, customers, trade associations, and industry standards organizations to collect information about competitors needs to be an explicit activity so that none of your business associates will feel your company has been operating in an unacceptable manner. To alleviate these issues, many benchmarking projects use a third-party consulting firm to gather performance measurement information at the beginning of a major benchmarking effort. This step is particularly helpful since it can be used to accelerate the search for appropriate world-class companies that allow you to conduct a site visit.

No matter how you approach this search phase, it is important to gain access to secondary sources and to develop a survey of performance benchmark measures across a target group of potential benchmark partners.

USING SECONDARY SOURCES

The Central Intelligence Agency collects much information about political, economic, and military interests in a wide variety of countries. In an article I read years ago, Richard Helms, a former director of the CIA, was quoted as saying that over 85 percent of all CIA research comes from appropriate analysis of the open literature. I was particularly impressed by that information and recalled it in 1987 when I was performing my first benchmarking study. That study was an investigation of a competing computer company to determine how progressive they were in their software development program. The literature search revealed an obscure article by one of their engineers that discussed their integration of structured analysis methods with quality function deployment to specify their software requirements. The entire benchmarking question was answered by an hour's research using a computer data base system. This experience convinced me that Helms's observation is equally true in the commercial world of benchmarking.

Perhaps the most important work on competitive intelligence and information gathering is Leonard Fuld's *Competitive Intelligence*.[4] Fuld identifies a wide range of secondary information sources.[5] A tool to help you begin your secondary research is presented in Figure 14.

Source Type	Where to Locate	Specific Resources
Computer Search	• Local public and university libraries • U.S. Department of Commerce — current industrial reports • Washington Service Bureau — GAO studies — congressional reports	• Key-word literature search • Access data sources — Dialog® — Dun and Bradstreet — Standard and Poor's — Value Line — Moody's Investment Service
Professional/ Trade Associations	• APQC Benchmarking Clearinghouse • Association for Manufacturing Excellence • American Marketing Association • The Strategic Planning Institute • *Encyclopedia of Associations*	• Industry-specific reports • Industrywide awards • Industry expert recommendations • Membership lists • Trade show exhibitors
Consultants/ Process Experts	• Referral by colleague • Professional association • Trade publication listing • *Bradford's Directory of Market Research Agencies and Management Consultants* • *Who's Who in Consulting* • *Directory of Management Consultants*	• Third-party industry surveys • References to individuals or data sources • Evaluation of search results

Figure 14. Secondary Data Sources

Figure 14 provides an overview of where to find and how to use services provided by libraries, associations, and consultant services for obtaining competitive information. The following steps outline a basic method for the information search process:

- Establish performance measures and data collection methods for the processes you have identified for comparison (use the same internal measures).
- Identify comparison organizations and secondary data sources (using the information developed using the methods described in Chapters 1 and 2).
- Collect information from secondary sources and quantify performance data.
- Simplify and reformat data in a way that identifies performance gaps.

Those four steps provide an outline for conducting secondary research. At the end of this process you should have identified all candidate benchmark-partner companies and collected data on their performance to compare against your internal process performance.

SUMMARIZING SECONDARY INFORMATION

The data search should result in a performance summary (by company) for each of the selected process performance measures. Each of the target companies of the benchmark study will have an interesting performance profile. Using a data presentation methodology similar to the process performance profile in Figure 12, summarize the information in a single table as in Figure 15. In this comparison chart the measures are listed in the left column, and the results for each company are recorded in their own dedicated column. The measures in Figure 15 represent a generic profile of company effectiveness for your form, use the performance measures you have selected for your specific process.

When you have exhausted all sources of external information, you are ready to propose the companies for the site visits. To determine which companies should be visited during the next phase of the benchmarking process, you will want to compare the information you have gathered to decide which companies exceed your company's performance in the chosen process. As you do this, consider the following questions:

- Do we have sufficient information to indicate that a performance difference exists?

Measure	Company Name		
1. Return on net assets			
2. Market share			
3. Debt-equity ratio			
4. Inventory (% sales)			
5. Revenue per employee			
6. Manufacturing overhead			
7. Capital interest (% sales)			
8. R&D (% sales)			
9. R&D investment efficiency			
10. New-product cycle time			
11. Forecast cycle time			
12. Order turnaround time			
13. Material lead time			
14. Production cycle time			
15. Customer response time			
16. Customer complaints (% shipments)			
17. Field returns (% shipments)			
18. Warranty rate (% sales)			
19. Parts returned to supplier			
20. First-pass yield			

Figure 15. Business Performance Comparison

- How recent and reliable is our information about this company?
- Are the similarities in the business of this proposed partner company sufficient to warrant a comparison with our company?
- Would any differences in the business of this proposed partner invalidate the comparison?
- Is this company likely to be willing to share the details of their process with us?

SELECTING BEST-IN-CLASS COMPANIES TO VISIT

Based on the analyses your team has conducted you are ready to enter the next phase of your search process: the formal request to benchmark the prospective partner companies you have identified. The first step in this process is to write a letter to the quality director or manager of the area you want to visit. In your request, be sure to focus the benchmarking study on a narrow topic and identify the particular sites or locations you wish to visit. You may also want to include a preliminary set of questions to help your prospective partner evaluate your study. Follow up this letter with a phone call to discuss your request in more detail and to determine the level of interest in this study.

It is particularly important to send your letter to the most appropriate manager at your target benchmark partner. Contacting the wrong person, may result in rejection, since busy managers may find it easier to reject a request than to pass it on to the appropriate individual. One company, for example, sent its request to the legal department because of their concern for developing a memorandum of understanding and disclosure agreement. Since the legal department was not intimately involved with benchmarking, it handled the request like any other contractual matter; it took three months to get the appropriate permission to do the study.

Although many companies are implementing benchmarking as a tool, there is no accepted model for developing this process. Thus, any particular targeted benchmark partner will probably have an approach different from your company's method for conducting a study. The negotiation period that follows the formal request allows both companies to coordinate their methods and establish a common approach to the proposed benchmarking study. Once both companies agree on the conditions of their study, then you are ready to enter into the observation phase.

CASE STUDY

Having defined their project in the plan stage, the Valiant Benchmarking Team needed to choose the companies to investigate. The management team had suggested Ford, Kodak and Xerox. The Valiant Team, however, decided to use the Benchmarking Clearinghouse to determine what companies were available to network with on the new product development process.[6] They discovered several other member companies known for research and development, and they identified Hewlett-Packard (HP), Intel, and Seiko as companies that had aggressive time-to-market performance. This was interesting, since this was the second time they had run across HP in their study. Through the clearinghouse, the Valiant Team identified the appropriate individuals to contact at each target company and gained cooperation to visit four companies: Ford, Hewlett-Packard, Intel, and Kodak. Each target company was selected from the electronics industry, rather than from a mechanical industry, since this would provide them with the best insight into their immediate competitive issues.

Their research, together with the input of their management team, indicated that they needed to understand what product features and service-performance levels were considered fundamental to their customers, where they could distinguish themselves from their primary competitors, and how they could deliver their product to market in record time. The team decided to divide the study in two: a product research effort to define the product in a way that would best meet the needs of their customers, and a process benchmarking study to evaluate what process improvements could reduce the time-to-market for this critical product.

The benchmarking team decided they would use the same approach with each of the companies visited and would try to conduct all the site visits during a two-week period, visiting a minimum of two divisions from each company. The same team would be kept intact for all visits and would prepare a consolidated report based on the revealed information. They communicated to the designated contact at each host company site the same set of questions to be covered during each eight-hour session:

1. What is your process for defining new product features?
2. How do you measure your product development teams?
3. What are the product review milestones that you use to indicate growth in maturity of the design?

4. What performance must be achieved at each of these milestones to receive approval to move to the next phase?
5. Do you use cross-functional teams for product development?
6. How are your project teams organized?
7. What is the role of each team member?
8. What companies are your role models for product development?
9. Is your current time-to-market adequate, and what are you doing to improve it?
10. What do you recommend we should read to learn more about competitive engineering practices?
11. How do you involve your suppliers in product design?

Exercise

Critique the above questions prepared by Martin. Would you make any changes? Is the team racing ahead too quickly in their study? Has the Martin team properly structured their strategic business situation to understand where they are going with this benchmarking project? How would you communicate these questions to the target benchmark companies?

Look again at the secondary data sources outlined in Figure 14. What other avenues would you check to complete your background investigations into these companies? Would it be helpful to the Valiant Team to complete the business performance comparison at this time — before visiting these companies? If you were facilitating their process, what would you recommend to the Valiant Benchmark Team as their next step?

NOTES

1. Ryuji Fukuda, *CEDAC: A Tool for Continuous Systematic Improvement* (Cambridge, Mass.: Productivity Press, 1989). CEDAC is the registered trademark of Productivity, Inc.

2. Examples of such strategic supplier alliances in the computer industry include companies like Conner Peripheral Products, Intel, and Microsoft, which provide parts or software to many companies in the industry and therefore have a unique perspective on the industry's function. Some of the industrial organizations include the American Electronics Association, Manufacturer's Association for Productivity and Innovation (MAPI), Semiconductor Advanced Technology (SEMATECH) Consortium, the Computer Business Executive Manufacturing Association (CEBEMA), and the Computer Systems Policy Project (CSPP) Council. Some stock-market analysts publish industry background surveys such as Kidder, Peabody, "Computer Systems Industry," *Equity Research Industry Report*.

3. "Competitive Intelligence: Everything You Always Wanted to Know About Your Competitors . . . But Were Afraid to Ask." *Industry Week* (Nov. 12, 1984) is an interesting article on competitive intelligence. This article quotes Leonard Fuld in his role as president of Information Data Search (IDS) of Cambridge, MA: "A survey [IDS] recently conducted for a client revealed that most companies don't keep track of what their employees tell outsiders. Because of managerial practices like these, it is never, ever impossible to get information." In the same article, Michael Kaiser of Kaiser Associates provides a list of eight guidelines for developing your own competitive intelligence department:

- Look at industry dynamics before you look at profit sheets.
- Target the most formidable competitors.
- Make your research focus clear.
- Get out from behind your desk.
- Don't computerize right away.
- Communicate results clearly.
- Conduct more than one search at a time.
- Make an analysis of your own company.

Kaiser concludes with the observation that "If competitor analysis is performed properly, there is no need to ever do anything immoral. Unethical practices can only give a company specific information, or facts, on the competitors. The key to competitor analysis, however, is the ability to go beyond the facts and anticipate how your competitors think. Facts usually reveal what your competitors have done in the past. What you want to know is how they're going to respond in the future." Another useful article: Richard F. Beltramini, "Ethics and the Use of Competitive Information Acquisition Strategies," *Journal of Business Ethics* (1986):5.

4. Leonard M. Fuld: *Competitor Intelligence, How to Get It, How to Use It* (New York: John Wiley, 1985) is the best source to begin understanding where to find secondary source materials. This book, along with Robert C. Camp, *Benchmarking: The Search for Industry Best Practices That Lead to Superior Performance* (Milwaukee: ASQC Quality Press, 1989) should be a mandatory reference in any company's library.

5. An interesting perspective of benchmarking is expressed in Richard Meyer, "Preserving the 'WA,'" *Financial World* (Sept. 17, 1991). It describes how benchmarking has been institutionalized — or made part of the nation's business network, in Japan. Meyer comments that a look at Asian philosophy makes it easy to understand why no one hoards a good idea. Japanese companies attempt to preserve the *wa* or group harmony — the process of working together although competitors. The Japanese nation works together as a team. Meyer's comment, "Today, the Japanese regard Americans as the world's worst benchmarkers," presents two basic truths. The first is that the American culture does not encourage teamwork the same way that the Japanese culture does. We tend to have an arrogance that comes from past business success. A second truth is that the Japanese are organized to benchmark in a way that American companies are not. For years, the Japanese External Trade Organization (JETRO) has been collecting commercial intelligence on the American market and sharing it among Japanese corporations.

6. See the Preface at Note 6.

4
Observing Best Practices

If you know the enemy and know yourself, you need not fear the result of a hundred battles. If you know yourself but not the enemy, for every victory gained you will also suffer a defeat. If you know neither the enemy nor yourself, you will succumb in every battle.

— Sun Tzu

SETTING THE TONE

Doing your homework is the first step toward a productive site visit. For one thing, the degree of your team's preparedness is immediately evident to your partner company, and making a professional impression on your first site visit is the best way to establish a good long-term relationship for future studies. Moreover, if your partner feels your team is unprepared or has not done its homework properly, they will be less likely to pursue any ongoing benchmarking relationship. Many partner companies with experience in benchmarking have recognized the need to limit their resources to those areas where they too can experience a payoff. Therefore, wasting your partner's resources on a low-productivity visit is not a good way to open your benchmarking relationship.

PLANNING THE VISIT

It is very important that you effectively plan your team's investigation before the site visit. The purpose of a site visit should be to verify the information you have researched and to clarify the process areas that were not fully described or that were difficult to understand. This approach basically follows the one used for the Malcolm Baldrige National Quality Award.[1]

Since benchmarking is a TQM tool, you will probably want to apply TQM in your process by involving all the team members in the planning and preparation tasks. In planning for your site visit, four basic tasks need to be performed once you have completed your research:

- Developing a site-visit strategy and questionnaire
- Preparing a data collection plan
- Agreeing with your partner on the ethics of the visit and the protocol for the visit
- Planning the logistics of the visit

Familiarizing your team with your partner's company is particularly important. The more familiar you are with the partner's business, the better you are able to manage your time during the site visit. In other words, don't waste time discovering things that you can read in open literature. Likewise, don't spend the limited time of a site visit attempting to make a cultural translation between your partner's business and your own. Thorough research eliminates this temptation and basic time-management problems.

Evaluating your partner's culture before the site visit also helps improve your team's ability to read the partner company's responses in the context of your own business culture. You may want to consider the following three aspects of business culture as initial key indicators of significant difference:

- The degree of formality of the business
- The degree of participation in their decision-making process
- The style of communication in their organization

Label the partner company's performance in each of these areas, then record your findings on the benchmarking partner analysis form in Figure 16.

Other information to know about your benchmarking partner includes the size of their business, the industry in which they operate, the type of ownership, the organizational structure, the style of manufacture (repetitive or process, just-in-time kanban or batch process), and your estimation of their core competencies. This information helps accurately interpret their process implementation and provides a better understanding of the underlying motivation and drive behind their decision process. The cultural analysis of your partner's company is discussed again in Chapter 6 (after the site visit, when this profile can be more completely modeled based upon your observations).

Once you have completed your background investigation, the next previsit tasks are developing a site-visit strategy and a data collection questionnaire, and making specific team assignments for executing the data collection plan. The site-visit strategy involves looking at a set of simple considerations:

- Do you want to conduct your questioning in small teams or in a large meeting?
- Do you want to have one lead interrogator or use a more democratic approach and rotate the questioning?
- Who is responsible for monitoring the time?
- Who will serve as the stenographer/scribe?

Measure	Company Name		
Business size:			
• sales revenue			
• number of employees			
Ownership of business			
Industry focus			
SIC code			
Organization structure			
Type of manufacturing			
Company culture:			
• formality			
• participation			
• communication			
Company competencies			

Figure 16. Benchmarking Partner Analysis

- Who will ensure that all questions are adequately covered?
- Do you want to visit particular areas in the company, have a general tour, or skip the plant tour completely and spend your time in a meeting room?
- Would you like to have particular people at the partner company, either by name or by job title, answer specific questions?
- Would you like to talk with a team that has conducted a particular project, or would you rather talk with their management?
- What evidence or supporting documents about their process (flowcharts, performance measurements, work instructions, etc.) would you like to see?
- Who will serve as your team leader, and who will be responsible for negotiating site-visit issues with a counterpart from your benchmarking partner?

The next major task in the data collection phase is to develop the questionnaire used during the site visit.

DEVELOPING A QUESTIONNAIRE

To stimulate your thinking about this subject, consider the generic benchmarking questionnaire in Figure 17, designed to guide you in developing your own. The questions presented fall into five major categories:

- Problem definition
- Process measurement
- Process problems
- Process improvements
- Process enablers

Notice that the first question in Figure 17 is an opening question. This type of question is used first to get your partners talking about something they enjoy — their successful process. Notice also that the questionnaire asks broad questions; this opens up communication and establishes a comfortable setting at the beginning of the visit. Making your partners feel comfortable and confident with your team is very important, especially if you expect to gain permission to probe deeper for specific answers using follow-up questions. Follow-up

1. How do you define this process? Please describe it.
   _____
   _____
   _____
   _____

2. Do you consider this process to be a problem or concern in your company? If not today, was it a problem in the past?
   _____
   _____
   _____
   _____

3. What is the measure of quality for this process? What are the criteria that you use to define excellence in process performance? How do you measure the output quality of this process? How do you measure progress in quality improvement?
   _____
   _____
   _____
   _____

4. How do you consider cost and schedule in this process?
   _____
   _____
   _____
   _____

5. How much and what type of training do you provide for the various job categories of the process team?
   _____
   _____
   _____
   _____

6. What process improvements have given you the best return in performance improvements?
   _____
   _____
   _____
   _____

7. What company, excluding your own, do you believe is the best in performing this process?
   _____
   _____
   _____
   _____

Figure 17. Benchmarking Questionnaire

questions, although not included on the questionnaire, are used to get to deeper issues and to clarify what the partner discloses. Keep in mind that the way you present your follow-up questions will indicate the degree of preparation you have put into this visit.

While uncovering performance measures and their trend values during your site visit may be an obvious task, the necessity for recording a description of recognized process enablers may be less apparent.[2] Process enablers provide you with the information needed to implement the benchmarking practice. While the performance measures indicate that the measure was successful, process enablers tell you the reasons behind the successful implementation: the system, method, document, training, or technique that facilitates the successful implementation of the benchmarked process. One of these process enablers is training — ensuring that those involved in the process acquire the knowledge and skills necessary for success. (For instance if you are studying benchmarking practices, you would want to know about their benchmarking training course.) In addition to training, process enablers can fit into several categories:

- Individuals' roles in the process (mentor, scribe, facilitator, etc.)
- The team's role in making decisions about their practice
- Data monitoring and collection systems
- Software that supports the practice
- Communication, recognition, and support functions that reinforce the process

After looking at all these considerations and working through the implications of each, you are ready to develop the specific set of questions to use on the site visit. Remember what was said earlier about questioning techniques: open-ended questions result in roundtable discussions (for example, the first question on Figure 17), whereas close-ended questions are used to capture specific information by eliciting a "yes" or "no" response or a selection from a limited number of answers. Because these questions tend to be abrupt and can increase tension when used improperly, it is particularly important to try to limit closed questions to specific data requests.

Asking for a scale of importance or priority is a technique used to obtain sensitive information without getting specific data. For instance, you can ask about the importance of cost (offering in situations a selection of very important, important, somewhat important, or not important) when asking about specific cost considerations may be difficult (e.g., manufacturing overhead).

Before you disclose the questionnaire to your partner company, test it in a real-world situation within your company. Don't use the questionnaire for a site visit unless it has been tested and evaluated using the following considerations:

- Does the questionnaire help guide your team to the knowledge that it seeks?
- Are the questions understandable — do they use common terms to make a single, clear request?
- Is it possible to answer the questions in a reasonable time?
- Is there any reason why your partner would not want to answer any of the questions?
- Does the sequence of these questions lead to the most open discussion?

Once you are satisfied with your set of questions, you should consider discussing them with the team leader's counterpart at your partner company. This is also a good time to discuss your site visit strategy information, ethical and protocol considerations, and specific travel details about your visit. You probably should consolidate your discussion of these items into one or two phone calls as a follow-up to your initial written agreement to conduct the benchmark study.

OBSERVING ETHICAL GUIDELINES

It is exceptionally important that you not misrepresent yourself while conducting a study. If any shadow hangs over benchmarking, it is the specter of industrial espionage; this is, in fact, one reason why the Benchmarking Clearinghouse at APQC is developing a code of ethics for benchmarkers.

One company, during a presentation of their research at a conference, mentioned the name of their benchmarking partner and described their performance on a particular process. Only after the conference did the partner company find out that their information had been divulged. Although probably done out of naivete rather than deliberate malice, this divulgence was inappropriate. Some additional practices to avoid include the following:

- Misrepresenting your company name, title, or reason for interest
- Collecting proprietary information without appropriate permission from all parties (including your company's legal counsel)
- Enticing others to give information in exchange for business
- Discussing the pricing of competitive products

During the course of benchmarking, partners may become privy to privileged information, even if it is not identified as confidential. For these reasons, a specific agreement needs to be made about ethical issues such as sharing information and confidentiality of the study results. Most companies are much more willing to discuss issues and concerns with those outside their industry than with direct competitors. This preference makes confidentiality even more important, since you cannot always be aware of the sensitive aspects of an industry unfamiliar to you.

There are some fundamental ethical guidelines appropriate to benchmarking. Perhaps a basic guideline is the golden rule: Don't do to your competitors or partners what you wouldn't want them to do to you. A second part to that rule also applies: Don't do anything that could cause your competitors or partners to sue! I strongly recommend that you have your corporate legal counsel draft a set of ethical principles to follow during benchmarking.

Agreeing on these ethical issues as well as on sharing information and confidentiality of results should be part of your pre-site visit negotiation with your benchmarking partner.

The comfort level of sharing the benchmark subject for both parties needs to be established. A basic rule is to avoid asking your partners to provide you with information about their companies that you would be unwilling to disclose about yours. You want to create an open atmosphere of trust that encourages communication. Another agreement that needs to be made explicit is the number of sites visited within each company and the frequency and duration of each visit. One discovery you will make is that best practices frequently differ from site to site or from division to division. The partner company itself may not have conducted internal benchmarking visits to understand the various local implementations of their practice.

Your detailed research may uncover real site-to-site differences in your partner company's practices of which they are not totally aware. One value-added contribution that you can offer them is the knowledge of what information has been published about their practice. Most companies are unaware of what has been published about their operations. Since many companies do not require management approval of articles published in technical journals, providing an external perspective of a company can be most helpful for clarifying their process self-knowledge.

The final aspect of pre-visit coordination is the logistical planning of travel arrangements and other requirements. Once all administrative and technical information has been communicated, you are ready to conduct the site visit.

CONDUCTING THE SITE VISIT

The fundamental purpose of a site visit is to collect information about the process you have selected for benchmarking. Concentrate on ensuring that all your questions are answered completely and that you have recorded this information in a way that you can use for developing your site visit report. To accomplish this objective, you must control your agenda and the time spent during the site visit. The objective is to get answers to your questions, not to participate in a social event. This means that you will need to keep track of your planned agenda and your progress in conducting your investigation.

The tone of the site visit should be cordial and professional. It is considered a basic practice that companies exchange information during benchmarking visits. This *quid pro quo* arrangement helps perpetuate the relationship between companies.[3] Once a relationship has been established and both companies have learned lessons that they feel are worthwhile, then you will have established the basis for a long-term information exchange that leads to continuous learning for both companies. In any case, having a successful site visit will require both companies to have a positive experience during this first visit. The following are some guidelines for a successful site visit:

- Schedule frequent breaks to caucus with your team and ensure that you are covering all areas. Find out if the team feels they are getting the data they need, and follow up on any area of questioning that requires more detail.
- Make midcourse corrections when you observe profound differences from the background information you have uncovered during your preliminary research.
- Ensure that the verifications and clarifications needed are obtained during the visit and that any additional information you need is clearly requested and agreed on before leaving the site.
- Act as a team during the site visit. Let all members participate equally in the questioning, and don't let one team member monopolize the visit.

RECORDING THE DATA

Dr. Noriaki Kano, the member of the Union of Japanese Scientists and Engineers (JUSE) who helped lead Florida Power and Light to their Deming Prize in 1989, observed that American business does not manage by fact — it "manages by gut." He has observed that American management is not proficient in the application of scientific methods to process improvement. Your basic data collection method is guided by using the questionnaire during the site visit to capture concrete data about the process you are studying.

The fundamental data focus of benchmarking is on collecting information from external and internal sources about your partner company and on identifying performance gaps. The reason you want both external and internal data is to assure that you obtain a consistent picture of their process. Consistency is developed only when your data collection method is solid.

A data collection plan may not be part of the initial benchmarking survey work; however, if it has not been developed before the site visit, the team may miss some opportunities for gaining some important data. The data collection plan helps you decide the why, what, when, how, and how much of the process to measure. By addressing these questions, your team will be able to agree on the approach they need to take for data collection. The questions to be asked in these areas include the following:

- *Why?* Since you will generate a lot of information about your target company, it is important to keep this information organized from the very beginning of your study. You need to be able to trace each measure of process performance from your internal benchmark of the process to the benchmark data from your partners. Without this built-in measurement correlation, you will not be able to do a good job conducting your performance gap analysis. A clear rationale for the data collected helps keep you on track.

- *What?* The specific data you keep should be readily understandable and easy to interpret. If you gather esoteric information, data that doesn't make sense out of context, or disjointed information, then you create more difficulties for your team as you attempt to interpret this information in your analysis. You should group data into the process steps and understand which factors exert a causal effect on the process performance and which are the process enablers. In addition to relevance, your information must be timely and reliable. Old or questionable information has little economic value in benchmarking. Indeed, it often creates a smoke screen of confusion for the analysis phase.

- *Who?* The team should be assigned to collect the data and to be aware of data collection opportunities during the site visit. One way to assign individuals to collect data is to give the data elements to those individuals most familiar with that information or process. This helps to sort the "wheat from the chaff" and makes it less likely that your partner company will present you with unusable information.

- *When?* Data should be collected in a timely manner. However, you must also determine which data should be collected from external sources and which data should be collected during the site visit. If you use a common set of measures to compare your process with your benchmark partner's, then you will also want to establish the appropriate measures for both the current level of performance and trend analysis, as well as for using this information to predict future performance levels.
- *How?* Using check sheets, job aids, and specific forms helps ensure the completeness of the information that is processed from your data.
- *How Much?* To determine the amount of data required, you will need to evaluate the scope of your project, figure out the number of potential sources of information, and decide how much that information could change if obtained from different sources (for instance, from multiple divisions of a single manufacturer).

The earlier these questions are addressed, the better your data collection efforts. The reason for explicitly addressing these questions will become evident as we enter our next step in the benchmarking process: analyzing performance gaps.

CASE STUDY

The members of the Valiant Benchmarking Team reviewed their questionnaire and realized they had not inquired about the use of goal setting in the development process. They decided to add questions about schedule goals and reliability goals to their survey.

Even though this was a tightly defined project, they had not anticipated that it would take two months to arrange for the business clearances and coordinate the site visits. They organized eight site visits over a continuous two-week period, scheduling one site visit with each of the four companies during the first week and visiting another division of each company in the second week. They scheduled the visits so their travel followed a logical sequence among the various sites.

During the first two site visits, they discovered that they had not developed a good strategy for pursuing follow-up questions. Their prepared questions did focus the opening discussion with the company project experts, however, and by the third site visit they had a working system for probing for more detail. After each day's visit, they convened for an hour and a half to discuss their observations.

Friday of each week was left open to consolidate the week's observations and to begin formulating their findings. During their first Friday session, the team realized they had observed a number of tools and approaches that they had not previously considered as potential enablers for the product delivery process:

- Quality function deployment
- Simultaneous engineering
- Early involvement of suppliers
- Teamwork among cross-functional groups
- Break-even time as a measurement
- Design of experiments to understand critical parameters for statistical control during product manufacture
- Reliability and service goals to focus the team's efforts

The team decided that these enablers could be used during the second week to focus their follow-up discussions.

Exercise

How would the benchmarking partner analysis form (Figure 16) have helped to focus the Valiant Team during this phase of their study? What would you have done differently?

During the site visits, the team discovered that the Management Roundtable had conducted a Survey of Product Development Practices, which evaluated 446 responses from 11 different industries.[4] What does this discovery suggest about the search phase of the Valiant Team's project? How do you think the partner company perceived this team? Does the information you have seen indicate that they are being professional? How would you recommend they improve their professionalism?

NOTES

1. *Update*, published by the American Society for Quality Control, is the official newsletter for the board of examiners of the Malcolm Baldrige National Quality Award. The August 1991 issue covers site visit guidelines. You may want to consider treating your benchmarking site visits with the same degree of professionalism that a team of Baldrige examiners uses for their site visits. The Baldrige team's process is certainly one of the best benchmarks for site-visit professionalism and preparation. Prior to a Baldrige site visit, each member of the team has probably spent between 30 and 40 hours in individual and group preparation, studying and evaluating the proposal, developing a consensus review, preparing the site visit issues, and planning the agenda of the visit itself.

2. Bob Camp, *Benchmarking*, 196, makes an excellent point when he distinguishes between enablers and benchmark practices. An enabler is a system, method, document, training, or technique that allows the successful implementation of a benchmarking practice. For instance, a benchmarking practice may be the use of QFD in the design process. Enablers for this process might include training in QFD software to support building the house of quality and the use of team facilitators to help coordinate the application of QFD in this project. Your team needs to make different decisions relative to benchmark practices and to the enablers. The first level of decision is for the benchmark practice: Do you want to use QFD in your design process? The second decision level is considered only after you decide to proceed: How do you want to implement QFD?

3. *Quid pro quo*, from the Latin, means an exchange of this for that. The basic understanding is that companies will exchange information about processes that they interpret to have equal value.

4. The Management Roundtable, *Survey of Product Development Practices* (Boston: 1991). A much earlier study that the team should have discovered involves Project Sappho (Scientific Activity Predictor from Patterns of Heuristic Origins), which is an examination of the difference between successful and unsuccessful R&D projects taken from two industries, chemicals and scientific instruments. See Center for the Study of Industrial Innovation, *Success and Failure In Industrial Innovation* (London: University of Sussex, 1972). It indicates that successful innovators have a much better understanding of the needs of their end users or customers.

5
Analyzing Performance Gaps

The general who wins a battle makes many calculations in his temple before the battle is fought.

— Sun Tzu

EVALUATING THE SITUATION

What do you do after the glamour of the site visit has passed? The post-site visit phase of benchmarking is a return to the general's tent to understand the root cause of process performance differences, and the effect of identified performance and process gaps.

Winning generals not only perform calculations in their tent, but today they also conduct "what-if" simulations to predict the alternatives among their business movements.[1] Jay Forrester, of the Massachusetts Institute of Technology, built an enterprise simulation model called Dynamo in the 1960s to evaluate alternative industrial scenarios in a continuous flow environment of business and economics.[2] Forrester's model examines management holistically, interrelating the flows of information, materials, staffing, money, and capital equipment. While he had to run his model on the most powerful computers of that day, today, models can be developed and analyzed on a personal computer.

Developing the most appropriate analysis tools to provide a complete picture of the situation is still an aspect of benchmarking that is evolving. Although sophisticated tools are under development at some of the more advanced benchmarking companies, it is not necessary to have these tools to get the major value out of a benchmarking project. Simple quality methods like data stratification, cause-and-effect analysis, relationship diagrams, and affinity diagrams provide you with the basic analysis capability you need for benchmarking.

In a few cases, however, you may need advanced statistical techniques such as methods to analyze more complex relationships, multivariate statistics, and experimental design. In this chapter, data stratification and root-cause analysis methods are explained and references are provided for the remaining methods, which are beyond the scope of a basic benchmarking project.[3]

STRATIFYING THE DATA

Data should be segmented according to appropriate, distinct subgroups. This method, called data stratification, helps identify sources of variance and indicates correlations among the trends. The stratification of data also permits observation of performance and process differences more quickly. One technique that is helpful for stratifying data is a special type of root-cause analysis using the cause-and-effect, or fishbone, diagram (sometimes called Ishikawa diagrams in honor of their originator, the quality control pioneer, Kaoru Ishikawa). This application is illustrated in Figure 18.

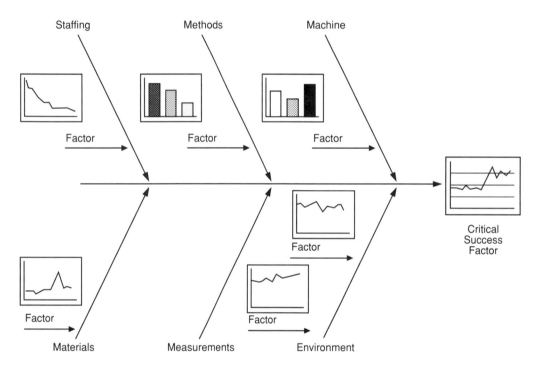

Figure 18. Root-Cause Analysis

In a standard cause-and-effect diagram, the effect is indicated at the head of the diagram and the potential causes are depicted on the skeleton to the left. The modified fishbone diagram uses data to understand correlating relationships among the potential causal variables. Instead of merely labeling root causes, the measures of performance for each of these variables is illustrated to indicate the actual performance of that variable. This is a graphic method for a multivariate analysis. Instead of confounding the analysis with numerical factors that relate each of the potential relationship strengths, this method graphically shows the relationships among the trends.

This method of cause-and-effect diagramming allows you to build an intuitive understanding of the many relationships you have observed, and it also provides strong visual clues to interrelationship possibilities. This method does not, however, expose possible confounding variables. If your analysis has a large number of variables whose relationship to the change is unclear, you should follow up this analysis with a more sophisticated analysis using design of experiments, analysis of variance, regression analysis, or multivariate analysis. These analytic tools will give you the most complete test results for comparing business and process factors.

PROJECTING THE GAPS

The basic tool for analyzing performance and process gaps is a table with a list of performance measures for each company measured as well as for your own company's performance (see Figure 15). Using this format, many of the performance and process gaps — things your partner does that you don't do — are evident immediately. Other gaps are less evident but will be revealed as you compare your internal process performance measures and documentation with that of your partner companies.

In evaluating these gaps, use Forrester's holistic approach and consider all flows that influence the process. Review material movement as well as data, control, and resource flows. Determining today's absolute level of performance, however, is less important than understanding what comprises the trend in that performance. Instead of aiming at today's target when you set up your action plan, you should project the benchmark into the future to understand what level of performance will be required and what enablers may help you attain that level.

Bob Camp describes the gap analysis well, and, in fact, the Xerox model is best-in-class among the benchmarking approaches for gap analysis. Camp uses a Z chart to display historical trend information and to project from the historical information estimates of future performance levels required to achieve competitive parity.[4] It is important to gain this type of understanding of future performance requirements and to integrate the benchmarked performance levels into your strategic planning process.

One caution is appropriate: benchmarks may be used for understanding the current best-performance achievements, and they are valuable for setting short-term goals or gaining commitments for improved levels of near-term performance; however, these same benchmarks are not valid for long-term use since the projections of future potential performance may not always follow the historical model. Improvement processes may result in continuous incremental gains (kaizen) or lead to strategic breakthroughs that leapfrog the competition (hoshin). You must remain alert for both continuous and breakthrough types of improvement potential. Many of the breakthrough improvements come from changing the business paradigm or from significant technological developments.

In any case, you must be cautious about applying linear thinking for projected goals. While a linear model is easy to understand and explain, the world does not always behave in a linear fashion, and linear goals sometimes become unrealistic. Any goal that you set should be tested for reasonability. As Dr. W. Edwards Deming advises, arbitrary numerical goals do not, of themselves, breed quality performance. The key to implementation of improvements is the discovery of process enablers.

IDENTIFYING PROCESS ENABLERS

In the preceding benchmarking step, we talked about recording information about both process measures and process enablers. An enabler is a system, method, document, training, or technique that facilitates the successful implementation of the benchmarked process.[5] While you have analyzed process performance measures in the benchmark gap analysis, you must also identify the key process enablers.

Key process enablers are those activities that facilitate the key behavioral or process changes; you identified those activities in the root-cause analysis as the stimulants of the performance change. This task of identifying enablers is actually a simple ranking of the enablers, assigning priority based on the information you receive in your interviews. All the information gathered about these key process enablers should be collected in the file that you maintain for each company you visit.

Although you need to fully understand process enablers, remember that enablement provides only the first element to support an effective change-management program. The second element is empowerment, and the final element is encouragement.

Empowerment is the act of providing individuals or teams with the power (fully delegated authority, responsibility, and resources) to act (evaluate, create, decide, implement, and express) in an environment of mutual respect and trust. Encouragement is the act of expressing appreciation, support, or formal recognition for the work done by individuals and teams. Encouragement does not need to be financial to be effective. When teams become the owners of their own process, their ability to follow through and implement their ideas and to learn by discovery as they focus on attaining the goals that they set is a strong reinforcement. In addition, words of recognition by management help strengthen feelings of accomplishment.[6]

These three E's — enablement, empowerment, and encouragement — are the responsibility of the management team to execute, because, unless you establish an enabling foundation, acts of empowerment and encouragement are meaningless to your employees. They will not be able to believe management's sincerity if you don't provide them with the things they need to "get the job done."

How should you introduce enablers to your employees after you have discovered them in your benchmarking process? Remember that Dr. W. Edwards Deming has warned over and over again to "adapt not adopt." You will need a thorough understanding of process obstacles or the potential barriers to implementing some other company's key process enabler in your company culture. That is the next step in your benchmarking process.

CASE STUDY

The Valiant Team gathered to evaluate the information they had collected during their two-week effort. They decided that the best way to understand trend information was to identify common practices at the four companies that differed from those at Martin Industries. They also decided to treat each of their partners' business sites as independent companies since the results of their study indicated that companywide practices were inconsistent across the divisions. They found they had obtained four major insights into their PDP that would improve their time to market.[7]

At Ford, they observed the trend to reduce the number of engineering changes before a product was released. They noted that their own practice was to make the product compatible with their manufacturing process during the first 90 days of production. Thus, most of their engineering changes occurred in that period. This difference allowed Ford to achieve design stability earlier in the product cycle than Martin could. The consequences of delayed design stability had many subsequent effects on suppliers to Martin. The enabler Ford cited that helped provide earlier focus for their design teams was a tool called quality function deployment, which, they said, had been perfected by Toyota several years before.

The Martin engineers found that Kodak's engineers had integrated their product-tooling strategy into the development process. Many of the long lead-time items required tools built by tooling engineers, and this tooling was always on the product's critical path. Kodak had discovered that by using simple tools to provide quick turnaround at the prototype stage (they called them "mud sets") and machining these parts to production quality, they could reduce the cycle time for tooling design. By using these parts to test many of the critical features, they could reduce the amount of time it took to release the hard-tooled or production-quality parts. The Martin team discovered they should have included a tooling engineer on their project team, and as a result they had not learned as much as they could from Kodak. Fortunately, Kodak was willing to host a follow-up visit with a Martin tooling engineer.

Intel provided them with an unexpected insight. Intel's design teams worked on product families, called chip sets, rather than on single design team projects. This idea came from their study of the Japanese camera industry where the designers planned a series of product introductions based on the progressive release of feature sets that their study indicated were needed by the public. Intel adapted this idea to the semiconductor industry and developed their team approach to 286-, 386-, 486-, and 586-series microprocessors around a similar concept.

The team discovered that Hewlett-Packard's staffing requirements for a design team were considerably different from Martin's. While HP staffed their teams with the appropriate types of project engineers, they also included representatives from manufacturing, marketing, purchasing, production control, accounting, and quality to assure that all operational areas were represented in the progressing maturity of the product development. Additionally, HP engineers were encouraged to gain experience in manufacturing and design, and management encouraged rotation among these assignments. One HP division even had production operators rotate as technicians into R&D to provide input on ease of product assembly. Martin took a different approach: the engineering team designed the product and transitioned it to operations on the date of product announcement. They calculated that this lack of involvement added an additional three months to the instability of the design.

Exercise

Did the Valiant Team conduct a true analysis of the nature, magnitude, and cause of the observed performance gap? How could you have improved their process for analysis? Using the model suggested for root-cause analysis, try to build the framework for the Martin study based on monitoring time-to-market as the effect. Does this analysis suggest some areas where Martin still has some lessons to learn (for example, other causes for time-to-market than those addressed)?

NOTES

1. Capers Jones of Software Productivity Research, Inc., in an unpublished paper dated April 15, 1988, cites some of the other characteristics of winning generals and compares these to attributes of losing generals as part of a study on military leadership. Many of these attributes transfer over into the analogy of business leadership. Winning generals tend to

   - Have self-confidence, innovativeness, and flexibility
   - Make personal observations of the situation and follow-up with rapid tactical movements
   - Acquire intelligence to explore opportunities
   - Plan operations at the campaign (strategic) and battlefield (tactical) levels
   - Appreciate the support issues of a major campaign and pay attention to logistics
   - Treat their troops and opponents fairly

   On the other hand, losing generals tend to have some flaw that leads to their defeat. Losing generals tend to

   - Make few independent decisions and have excessive reliance upon councils and subordinates
   - Repeat their same mistakes and be surprised by their opponents movements
   - Exercise caution and move slowly or sit in fixed emplacements
   - Select conservative tactics and weapons
   - Ignore basics of support and logistics, campaign planning, and tactical execution
   - Suffer communication breakdowns from their inability to coordinate their operations across a broad front
   - Treat their troops and opponents abusively

   I enjoyed Jones's observations and hope that you can see the intuitive analogy of competitive analysis and benchmarking in business.
2. Forrester's work is published in several volumes available through Productivity Press: *Industrial Dynamics* (Cambridge, Mass.: Productivity Press, 1961), *Principles of Systems* (Cambridge, Mass.: Productivity Press, 1968), *Urban Dynamics* (Cambridge, Mass.: MIT Press, 1968), *World Dynamics*

(Cambridge, Mass.: Wright-Allen Press, 1971), and *The Collected Papers of J.W. Forrester* (Cambridge, Mass.: Wright-Allen Press, 1975).

3. Books on these topics of data analysis include: Olive Jean Dunn and Virginia A. Clark, *Applied Statistics: Analysis of Variance and Regression* (New York: John Wiley, 1974), Donald F. Morrison, *Multivariate Statistical Methods*, 2nd ed., (New York: McGraw-Hill, 1976), George E.P. Box and William G. Hunter, *Statistics for Experimenters: An Introduction to Design, Data Analysis and Model Building* (New York: John Wiley, 1978), Lance A. Ealey, *Quality by Design: Taguchi Methods and U.S. Industry* (Dearborn, Mich.: ASI Press, 1988), and Tetsuichi Asaka and Kazuo Ozeki, eds., *Handbook of Quality Tools: The Japanese Approach* (Cambridge, Mass.: Productivity Press, 1990).

4. Camp, *Benchmarking*, 151-156.

5. See Note 2 in Chapter 4 for an expanded discussion of enablers.

6. This proposition is for a systemic solution to recognition and appreciation. In the classic book by Kenneth Blanchard and Spencer Johnson, *The One-Minute Manager* (New York: Berkley Books, 1983), the lesson is that even brief positive verbal expressions are highly appreciated by employees and result in their increased motivation. The reason for this response is that employees seldom hear that they are doing a good job. However, the motivation that comes from a "thank you for a job well done" is not as long lasting as the personal satisfaction that comes with the empowerment to manage your own job in a world-class manner *and then* hearing management's words of acclamation.

7. The need to focus on quality and its relationship to time-to-market is in Henry Ford, *Today and Tomorrow* (New York: Doubleday, 1926; Cambridge, Mass.: Productivity Press, 1988). Ford dedicates a chapter to managing time in which he draws the relationship between quality and time reduction (beginning on page 112). "It is not possible to repeat too often that waste is not something which comes after the fact. . . . Picking up and reclaiming scrap left over after production is a public service, but planning so that there will be no scrap is a higher public service." The most complete discussion of the relationship between quality, cost, and time-to-market is in George Stalk, Jr., and Thomas M. Hout, *Competing Against Time* (New York: Free Press, 1990).

6

Adapting Superior Practices
to Your Culture

Synthesizing Best Practices
Developing an Action Plan
Setting Goals
Managing Your Culture
Implementing the Plan
Gaining Organizational Support
Case Study

There is timing in everything. Timing in strategy cannot be mastered without a great deal of practice.

— Miyamoto Musashi

SYNTHESIZING BEST PRACTICES

Otto von Bismarck once said, "Fools you are . . . to say you learn by your experiences. . . . I prefer to profit by others' mistakes and avoid the price of my own." This is a pragmatic approach to warfare, whether military or commercial. This chapter focuses on applying your company's creativity to adapt best practices to your company culture. This step of the benchmarking process also includes communicating to your company the findings of the study and the work required to gain buy-in and the support needed for implementing these findings.

What does best practice really mean? Best-in-class, best-of-breed, world-class, industry leader: all these labels mean that the performance of the company you are benchmarking is recognized as the best among observable worldwide practices. These terms have become popularized by the press and have been used indiscriminately ever since Tom Peters introduced the topic of excellence in 1982. In the world of systemic benchmarking, this label has a rigorous, narrow meaning rather than a robust, broad meaning. The practice that is best-in-class should not be the one that is most advertised or most accessible to your analysts; neither should it mean the company that won the Malcolm Baldrige National Quality Award. After all, the best-in-class may not have applied for the award! Indeed, best-in-class may not exist at all for a particular practice, and you may have to develop a composite practice that reflects the input of many companies. At this stage of the benchmarking study, an action plan needs to be developed for your company. You will need to synthesize the process information you have gathered in a way that is appropriate for your company's culture.[1]

DEVELOPING AN ACTION PLAN

The action plan for implementing a particular enabler follows the general format of a *hoshin* plan.[2] Hoshin is a system for establishing process objectives and goals and implementing them through a set of strategies that are monitored at particular milestones to determine if the process is on target. Hoshin plans are used in Japanese businesses to manage strategic changes that result in breakthrough improvements in the company's management system. One indicator of the need for a "breakthrough improvement" is a significant gap in performance for the critical success factors of a key business process. Change to such a process is managed by the process owner.

For each process there is a process owner, either the individual or team responsible for the operation of that process. Process owners coordinate their process's functions and work activities. A process owner makes changes in the process as required, managing the entire process to ensure that it applies its sequence of value-added tasks to produce a high-quality output. A major responsibility of the process owner is to manage the efficiency, effectiveness, and economy of the process by eliminating waste. The process owner is also responsible for process improvement.

The form Figure 19 outlines for the process owner how to build a benchmarking action plan. At the top of the form, identify the key business process and define the critical success factor. Then indicate the date that the action plan is drafted and summarize the results of the benchmarking study. In the area labeled *objective*, define the change this action plan is to address, including the estimated date of completion and the desired level of performance in the critical success factor. Then record the short-term goals (six months to a year) and the longer-term goals (with the expected date of achievement). The benchmark is recorded with the date of observation, company name, level of performance, and rate of improvement.

In the last section of the form, describe the specific strategies needed for achieving the change. For each strategy, name the owner — individual or team — responsible for completion. Each strategy should also include specific schedule milestones for accomplishing a targeted level of performance.

SETTING THE GOALS

The form in Figure 20 provides one approach for monitoring process performance, which is a critical part of establishing your benchmarking goals.

Your benchmarking team needs to define the most appropriate measurement and data collection method for each critical success factor. This is done to ensure that you are measuring performance the same way at each benchmarked company. Figure 20 can be used to record performance over time at the top five companies in your benchmark study; it also provides a section to

Process: _____

_____

Critical Success Factor: _____

_____

Process Owner: _____ Date: _____

Summary of Study Results

Objective

Goals

Short-term

Long-term

Benchmark

Company: _____

Date Observed: _____

Level: _____ Rate: _____

Strategy (owner)

Targets and Milestones

Figure 19. Benchmarking Action Plan

Critical Success Factor: _____

Measurement Method: _____

_____

_____

Performance analysis (Top 5 Companies)   Date: _____

Company	Date	Level	Date	Level	Date	Level	Date	Goal
Self-analysis								

Best Observed Performance Level: _____

_____

Best Observed Sustained Rate of Improvement: _____

_____

Highest Stated Performance Goal: _____

_____

Recommended Short-term Goal: _____

_____

    Rationale: _____

_____

_____

Recommended Long-term Goal: _____

_____

    Rationale: _____

_____

_____

Figure 20. Establishing Benchmark Goals

record your own performance. This information helps you set realistic performance goals for your projects. By maintaining a historical file on process performance, you will be able to improve your goal-setting ability and to better determine which of your critical success factors are linear or nonlinear.

MANAGING YOUR CULTURE

Each company has a unique culture as determined by its management style and historical perspective.[3] There are at least four indicators of a company's culture: form of ownership, organizational structure, communication style, and degree of trust. These factors, outlined in the company cultural profile in Figure 21, suggest the degree of freedom that a company has in both implementing TQM and incorporating strategic change.

The first cultural distinction, the form of ownership, helps determine the extent of management buy-in that is required in a company. In a family business or a closely held organization, the dynamics of the business are more personal than in a *Fortune* 500 company. For this reason, implementing TQM in the larger organization is often easier because those individuals carry less personal and emotional baggage than employees of closely held or family businesses. The large corporation is less personal, however, and the actual implementation of TQM is most often challenging because of the difficulty in directly involving employees and recognizing their achievements. No matter where you are on this ownership scale, you will probably experience a small challenge in implementing changes that is a function of your unique culture.

Organizational structure, the second distinction, is also a significant factor in assessing a company's culture. Structure can range from simple to complex. At one end of the spectrum is a single site or single business unit, which is typical of a small business. At the other end of the organizational spectrum is a more complex multinational conglomerate. The business with a simple structure is likely to have a single culture or way of working together, while the business with a complex structure is likely to have as many cultures as it has operating units. The difficulty for the latter business is its inability to maintain relationships across divisional boundaries, although even a single business unit will have to deal with some "semi-cultural" boundaries, such as those between marketing, R&D, accounting, and manufacturing. Each of these areas may form a professional subculture that needs to be bridged. Whether large or

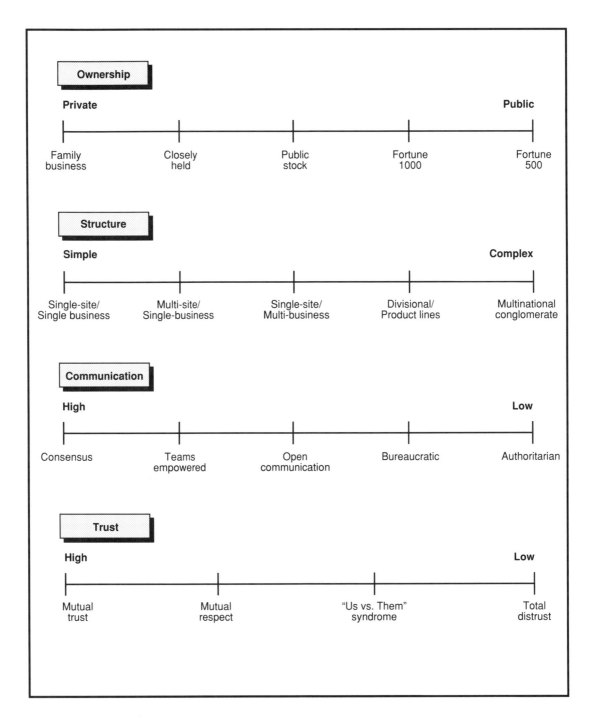

Figure 21. Company Cultural Profile

small, there are challenges in forging a seamless border between functional or organizational units. The manner in which this is done helps to characterize a company's culture.

A third distinction that helps define a company's culture is the functioning of its internal communications. This scale goes from a high-communication model in a consensus environment to a low-communication model in an authoritative, dictatorial model. Communication is the vehicle for sharing change initiatives and team successes; it is an indicator of the degree of "process ownership" that is applied to the business unit.

The final cultural distinction is the degree of trust. Trust is earned through experience; it is not given because of title or ownership. In a lower-trust environment you will observe a "we-they" syndrome where people do not act as part of the same team. At its extreme, low trust leads to total distrust of everyone. Hopefully, this is observable only among the inmates of certain classes of prison facilities. Mutual respect is based on technical competence and is actually a healthy form of culture. Mutual trust, however, is the highest degree of trust.

Although the management team is responsible for deciding on the most successful method for introducing change in their cultural environment, it is important to note that none of these four cultural distinction scales operates in isolation from the others. This is a perfect example of Forrester's model of the integrated effects in a dynamic system.[4] The reason for calling these considerations to your attention is that they are the determinants of success for any particular approach used in implementing a strategic change initiative as a result of a benchmark study.

Why should you perform a cultural analysis before implementing a strategic change? You do this to expose any barriers or obstacles to change and try to eliminate any noncultural elements from the process. This allows you to develop an implementation plan that gets the buy-in of all affected parties. This is TQM in action.

IMPLEMENTING THE PLAN

The structure of an implementation plan directly follows the action plan and applies techniques used for managing engineering projects.[5] Figure 22 illustrates an implementation plan for a particular strategy in a benchmarking action plan.

Process: _____

Process Owner: _____   Date: _____

Team Members: _____

_____

Strategy Statement: _____

_____

Activity	Owner	Schedule/Milestones						Performance	
		Month	Month	Month	Month	Month	Month	Target	Actual

Figure 22. Benchmarking Implementation Plan

The top section of the implementation plan contains information that allows it to be linked with the action plan and identifies the team members responsible for implementing this strategy. The strategy is then divided into activities and each activity is then assigned an owner who is responsible for developing the target performance. The form can also be used as a planning device for recording the estimated time to completion and milestone dates for performance. This follows the same methods used in a Gantt chart. As time passes, a second timeline is added beneath each estimated timeline on the plan to monitor and record the actual schedule of task progression. This permits side-by-side presentation of estimated and actual schedule performance. The target performance level is then compared to the actual performance level in the right-hand column.

GAINING ORGANIZATIONAL SUPPORT

As mentioned earlier, to successfully implement strategic change, it is necessary to gain the buy-in of all affected parties. Securing management's support is an obvious requirement; however, getting the endorsement of those groups and individuals who are directly affected by the change in their daily work habits is more frequently forgotten. Yet it is the individuals closest to the process who are most capable of assessing the value of a proposed change. Keep in mind that one principle of TQM states the importance of involving employees in the decisions that affect them. You may well be able to eliminate some barriers to change by allowing the employees in the target key business process to work on improving the ideas that were generated by the benchmarking study. That will be the final step in your benchmarking process.

CASE STUDY

After preparing a benchmarking action plan (see Figure 23), the Valiant Team decided to merge its observations and suggest to Martin management a new approach to product development. The members of the benchmarking team liked the HP project team's cross-functional concept and also discovered that Apple, IBM, and Motorola have used a similar approach for fast-track product developments. They suggested that the Valiant team project team use a tool like quality function deployment for developing a product family of new-generation cash registers to meet the projected needs of their customers (linking this idea to the effort of the other study team that is focusing on product features). They also liked the use of a tooling strategy to help reduce the impact of tool-building time on the project's critical path. The Valiant Team began to write up these recommendations into a briefing for senior management.

Exercise

Review the summary of study results on the benchmarking action plan. Does it accurately reflect the results of the study that should be communicated to senior management? How would you rephrase the objective to indicate time-frame and degree of improvement desired? What could be improved in the statement of the goals, targets and milestones? Where would you look to understand the detail in each strategy area?

What company cultural considerations should be made for adapting these best practices into Martin Industries? How would the company cultural profile (Figure 21) aid in identifying potential obstacles for the action plan? How would you state the objective for the Valiant Team? Do you have enough information to draft an action plan?

Process: _____Product Delivery Process_____

Critical Success Factor: _____Time-to-Market_____

Process Owner: _____Sr. V.P. R&D_____ Date: ___11/25/91___

Summary of Study Results

Survey conducted of Ford, Kodak, Intel and Hewlett-Packard indicates the use of cross-functional teams, quality function deployment and a critical-path-reducing tooling strategy.

Objective

Implement product delivery strategies that will enhance the product's time-to-market indicator.

Benchmark

Company: _____HP (Printer)_____

Date Observed: ___11/15/91_____

Level: _22 months_____ Rate: _decreasing_

Goals

Short-term

1. Conduct QFD Analysis of the new Valiant product by 1/31/92
2. Develop a more representative team for the Valiant project.

Long-term

1. Revise the new product delivery process to reduce the time to market. Implement by end of next fiscal year.

Strategy (owner)

1. Implement QFD (Smith)

2. Revise Valiant Team membership to reflect all cross-functional areas (Riley)

3. Develop and implement a product tooling strategy (Lambert)

Targets and Milestones

Complete by 1/31/92

Complete by 12/15/91

Complete by 3/1/92

Figure 23. Benchmarking Action Plan

NOTES

1. In the report of the MIT Commission on Industrial Productivity an observation is made about best practice: the firms that lead in their industries have a similar attitude about business innovations — they view them as a coherent package of changes rather than as independent solutions to particular problems. The commission mentions several of these business innovations: benchmarking, team-based approaches to process management, emphasis on customer satisfaction, a focus on flatter organizations, employee involvement in decision making, profit sharing, and a commitment to training and continuous improvement. Each of these business innovations has features that reinforces the others. Indeed, these are the elements of TQM. This report is by Michael L. Dertouzos, Richard K. Lester, Robert M. Solow, et al. *Made in America: Regaining the Productive Edge* (Cambridge, Mass.: MIT Press, 1989).

2. The planning process suggested here is similar to the hoshin planning process. Three books will help you learn more about hoshin. The historical development of this planning method is covered in Yoji Akao, *Hoshin Kanri*, (Cambridge, Mass.: Productivity Press, 1991). An implementation model for hoshin is contained in my book, *Managing by Consensus* (working title) (Cambridge, Mass.: Productivity Press, forthcoming). Bob King, *Hoshin Planning: The Developmental Approach* (Methuen, Mass.: GOAL/QPC Press, 1989), presents the seven Japanese management tools in their hoshin planning context.

3. Allen L. Wilkens, *Developing Corporate Character* (San Francisco: Jossey-Bass, 1989), 39, observes that: "When organizations develop a unique competence, the relevant people will know how to perform the complex behaviors involved, but they often will be unable to tell you everything that is required to perform the skill because it will have become second nature." Essentially, they have become too close to their process to see it objectively, and the practice itself is too ingrained to examine critically. Once a process has become rote, it is likely to suffer from the laws of entropy and begin a degradation phase.

4. See Chapter 5, Note 2.

5. Critical path method (CPM), performance evaluation review technique (PERT), and Gantt charts (named after Henry Gantt, who developed this method in the early 1900s) are used for scheduling and tracking engineering

projects. These methods are even emulated in the arrow diagram, one of the seven new Japanese management tools (see Asaka and Ozeki, *Handbook of Quality Tools*, cited in Chapter 5, Note 3). These techniques are discussed in Harold Kerzner, *Project Management: A Systems Approach to Planning, Scheduling, and Controlling*, 3rd ed. (New York: Van Nostrand and Reinhold, 1989) and George J. Ritz, *Total Engineering Project Management* (New York: McGraw-Hill, 1990). The editors of the *Harvard Business Review* have drawn together some articles on project planning in their anthology *Managing Projects and Programs* (Cambridge, Mass.: Harvard Business Review Press, 1989). In particular, two of these reprints are of interest: "The ABC's of the Critical Path Method" by Ferdinand K. Levy, Gerald L. Thompson, and Jerome D. Wiest (1963), and "How to Plan and Control with PERT" by Robert W. Miller (1962).

7

Improving Process Performance

To renew when we are deadlocked with the enemy means that without changing our circumstances we change our spirit and win through a different technique.

— Miyamoto Musashi

USING TEAM CREATIVITY

Renewal during battle is important to a warrior. This means that the warrior finds encouragement during the battle when the natural tendency is to experience depression. In business, finding renewal in the midst of the chaos of the struggle is likewise important. A principal source of renewal is the reinforcing power of the team structure. By taking implementation plans for strategic change to the teams for review and approval you obtain something more powerful than their concurrence: you obtain their creative input.[1]

The power of a consensus approach to management is in listening to the ideas, opinions, and perspectives of a variety of people; gathering data together and examining its meaning; and agreeing on the best way to integrate all these sources of information into a plan that all members can support. Using team creativity means that you have applied a different technique — the power of consensus — to improve on the best practice of your partner company. Benchmarking has a bias toward action — the implementation of results that will change your business. Your job is not complete simply because you have identified a best practice and developed an action plan. The competitive business environment demands continuous monitoring of process improvements to evaluate the results of those implemented changes on process performance. Merely performing the implementation plan is not enough, you need to assess your progress by reviewing it regularly. This is the check step of plan - do - check - act (PDCA).

The PDCA cycle is the universal management process and a fundamental principle of TQM. TQM not only sets goals but also measures and reports progress as you move toward your goal. Part of process improvement comes from paying attention to the implementation of the best practice.[2] The first step is recording the data.

MAPPING THE HISTORICAL TREND

It is important to record the results of your process improvement efforts. This record helps in calibrating your efforts against the ongoing improvements made at your partner company. A prudent company will also track this performance relative to their industry performance. The historical-trend graph in Figure 24 is a suggested format for tracking and comparing industry average performance against your company's performance and that of the benchmark. Notice that the chart changes in the time scale to show the last three quarters of performance, and then it displays the individual results of each month in the current quarter.

An organization must learn from its change initiatives. In *The Fifth Discipline*, Peter Senge uses a systems approach to building a learning organization.[3] Senge suggests the following laws that apply to almost any change implementation and that form a set of valid considerations for monitoring our study progress:

- Today's problems come from yesterday's solutions.
- The harder you push, the harder the system pushes back.
- The cure can be worse than the disease.
- Faster is slower.
- Cause and effect are not closely related in time and space.
- Small changes can produce big results — but the areas of highest leverage are often the least obvious.
- Dividing an elephant in half does not produce two small elephants.

Senge's work suggests that many businesses need to overcome their learning disabilities and use team learning to develop the group thinking that will lead to the achievement of shared visions. This is also the goal for implementing strategic-change initiatives through benchmarking.

TRACKING SUCCESS FACTORS

If you are implementing an action plan across many organizations, it may be helpful to monitor their progress and compare any modifications they have made to the basic process enablers. The tracking form in Figure 25 can be used to monitor the progress of multiple sites. Completing this form for each review period allows you to observe changes in performance (current level) and goals. The section at the bottom is for recording differences in process enablers.

Process: _____

Process Owner: _____ Date: _____

Qtr./Yr.   Qtr./Yr.   Qtr./Yr.   Mo./Yr.   Mo./Yr.   Goal
                                                              Qtr./Yr.

Key

| Industry Average | Company Performance | Company Goal | World Class |

Figure 24. Benchmark Historical Trend

Critical Success Factor:	Performance			Benchmark
Location	Current level	Short-term goal Year	Long-term goal Year	Company: Date:

Performance Enablers
Short-term:
Long-term:

Figure 25. Critical Success Factor Tracking

COMPLETING THE CYCLE

Benchmarking's six steps parallel the four steps of PDCA (see Figure 5). What do you do when you complete a study? You go back to the beginning and repeat the benchmark study to recalibrate the results. Renewing your benchmarking efforts will allow your team to track the progress of your benchmarking partners in their improvement of critical success factor performance, and to observe changes in their processes as they adjust to changing business conditions.

CASE STUDY

Martin's management team agreed with most of the Valiant Team's recommendations, but management wanted further specifics on the tooling process. However, they were uncomfortable with the blatant theft of ideas from other companies because they were unsure as to whether these ideas would work for them. They decided to require frequent project reviews to ensure that these new approaches to product development would not result in a lengthened time-to-market.

The Valiant Team leader objected to these frequent reviews because he felt that they would bog down the team in a morass of paperwork. He suggested that the management team observe the functioning of the Valiant Team on a regular basis by frequent visits to their location. He added that this would greatly boost the morale of the employees. He cited the morale-building efforts of management at Data General as one of the keys to their early success. He also noted that Hewlett-Packard management practiced "management by wandering around" and that their senior managers were known to wander into the engineering areas to check out the progress on new product designs.[4]

Exercise

What is the value of the regular review process for this change effort? Do you support the team leader's observation that these process reviews would "bog down the team in a morass of paperwork"? Has the Valiant Team improved on the ideas that they observed and felt worthy of adaptation to Martin? Have they considered all possible process improvements?

NOTES

1. Innovation and creativity are two sides of a coin — both can be used to help overcome the inertia of a stagnant organization. Creativity refers to the insightful development of new ideas, and innovation refers to the implementation of these ideas. This definition is from William C. Miller, *The Creative Edge: Fostering Innovation Where You Work* (New York: Addison-Wesley, 1987). An old saying defines the need for creativity: "If you do what you've always done, then you'll get what you've always got." Tradition is being stuck in the same place — a repetitive cycle that does not lead to true progress. The strategic change that flows from benchmarking is aimed at improving on tradition. Other books on this topic include R. Donald Gamache and Robert L. Kuhn, *The Creativity Infusion* (New York: Harper & Row, 1989) and William C. Byham, *Zapp! The Lightning of Empowerment* (Pittsburgh: Development Dimensions International Press, 1988).

2. The principles of continuous improvement are found in Masaaki Imai's *Kaizen* (New York: Random House, 1986). This book is now available through McGraw-Hill.

3. For more information on the learning organization see Peter M. Senge, *The Fifth Discipline: The Art and Practice of the Learning Organization* (New York: Doubleday Currency, 1990).

4. Management by Wandering Around (MBWA) was developed as a cultural aspect of Hewlett-Packard's management practice. Tom Peters and Nancy Austin revealed MBWA to the public in *A Passion for Excellence: The Leadership Difference* (New York: Random House, 1985). It is interesting to note that benchmarking is a form of MBWA.

8

Seeking the Horizon

If you are thoroughly conversant with the enemy's strategy, you will recognize the enemy's intentions and thus have many opportunities to win.
— Miyamoto Musashi

BENCHMARKING AS A PROCESS

What do you do after the benchmarking study is done? According to most practitioners, you recycle the study to recalibrate the results and continue your process improvement. And they are right. Since benchmarking is a process, it is essential to reiterate the process. Not only are business conditions always changing, but also new entrants are always seeking a market opportunity that has been left exposed. For benchmarking to work in your company, it needs to be a commitment to a long-term change management effort.

Effective long-term change management begins with your company's pursuit of a sequence of objectives, like a hiker following a series of blazes along a wilderness trail. Navigating this journey requires not one lone signpost, but rather a series of signposts that point the way to the ultimate destination. This is why one isolated benchmarking study does not produce the same value as a planned sequence of benchmarks.

In order to recognize the intentions of your competitors and generate opportunities to win, you must be thoroughly conversant with their strategy, their change capabilities, and their natural response to challenge. A continuing benchmark program supports your understanding of competitive moves within your industry. Even though your competitors will not allow you to observe their leading-edge developments, your benchmark partners may.

With the continuing reiteration of your benchmark studies, you improve the quality of the information you acquire and the reliability of your benchmarking results as well as the establishment of long-term relationships with truly excellent companies. These long-term relationships allow you to validate the projections you have made for future benchmark performance standards. Continuously reviewing your benchmarks will result in the ability to create a series of improvements that ultimately position your company as truly "world class." By maintaining long-term relationships with benchmark partners and recalibrating your measures, you generate the opportunity to win in your competitive battles.

SUPPORTING A BENCHMARKING PROGRAM

What does it take to support your benchmarking program over the long haul? There are five areas you may want to consider for developing your benchmarking activity. One of the first things necessary for a robust benchmarking program is a good *internal training program* that teaches your teams how to conduct a benchmarking study. Education changes thinking; training changes behavior, both are needed in benchmarking. Ways of thinking need to be changed in order to overcome the "not invented here" syndrome that plagues so many American companies and to accept that your team may not have all the answers. Behavior also needs to change to allow us to recognize the excellence that exists in other companies without becoming self-critical or boastful about our own capability.

A second support consideration is a *research library* to provide access to computerized data bases, to maintain the reports and files gathered during the benchmarking studies, to track the progress of benchmarking projects, and to house the collection of research materials.

Third, it is necessary to have a method, such as a *management information system*, for coordinating benchmarking team projects. This system describes ongoing activities and permits teams to discuss projects with each other; this also could be integrated with team tracking and the file of benchmarking study reports.

Fourth, both *internal and external networks* of individuals to facilitate your studies are needed. At Xerox, for example, an internal network meets at regular meetings and even publishes a newsletter of its activities. An external benchmarking network can provide you with a ready source of partners for specific studies.

The final aspect of an internal structure required for a robust benchmarking program is a cadre of *professional benchmarking analysts* to support critical studies and to facilitate teams in their benchmarking studies. Bring all of these elements together and you can form the foundation for a world-class benchmarking program.

PUTTING IT ALL TOGETHER

Benchmarking is particularly valuable for setting challenging yet realistic business goals because it provides a systematized method for improving key business processes. If your company does not conduct benchmarking, then you will never know how good your processes are, and you will never fulfill your true capabilities.

Another activity to do after the benchmarking study is review your benchmarking process. When you follow the continuous improvement process, the check step of the plan - do - check - act cycle requires that you ask how to improve the process, not just how to improve the results produced by the process. One way to seek continuous improvement in your methods is by *benchmarking, benchmarking!* Partnering with other firms on benchmarking studies, can help you expand your capability to benchmark by negotiating benchmark protocols and by observing how other companies conduct their benchmarking process.

Once benchmarking becomes integrated into your continuous improvement process, you will have the opportunity to realize increased performance on a regular basis. Many companies call this action *institutionalizing the process*. This means that the process is a part of your company's daily operations. At this stage of integration, benchmarking becomes as visible a TQM tool as strategic quality planning, product quality measurement, and customer satisfaction surveys.

APPLYING TQM TO BENCHMARKING

Benchmarking is a basic business tool for management; it reinforces the other quality tools that are used for implementing continuous improvement in all of the business processes. One factor that distinguishes the best firms from others is that they see the various business tools and systems not as independent solutions to a problem but as a coherent package of change mechanisms. These best firms take a systems approach to the design of their business, using TQM techniques to complement their strategic planning and business process improvement methods.[1] A fundamental recognition of these companies is that all company activities are composed of many interrelated processes. This is a TQM basic principle and a necessary precondition for quality thinking.

Another TQM basic principle is that every process can and should be understood, controlled, and improved. Since total quality applies to the entire organization, management needs to apply time and attention to understanding and improving the processes they supervise.

GOING BEYOND THE BOUNDARIES

So much activity is happening as this book is completed that it is difficult to summarize. Benchmarking is becoming a trend in America, but it is not a fad that will soon pass. It is absolutely essential to use this tool to succeed. Xerox has been using benchmarking effectively since the mid-1970s and Japanese companies have been using benchmarking even more successfully since the mid-1950s.

One obstacle that many companies need to overcome is an arrogance that states: "Our company has succeeded based on these principles or methods. Why should we taint ourselves by looking at other people's processes?" As George Romney once said: "Entrenched success breeds arrogance." We must guard against myopic views of our business and look at the bigger picture. Benchmarking opens our perspective by looking at other companies and their approach to similar problems.

What is most important to remember about is that benchmarking works. This means that you should not delay in your quest for the information you need to begin your process. Today, more companies are investigating the use of benchmarking in their improvement projects than ever before.[2] While there has been a significant increase in benchmarking interest and activity, I predict that the popularity of benchmarking will continue to rise in the next few years, as more companies see the value of benchmarking for stimulating improvement in their business. So, seize the day! Begin your benchmarking process now!

CASE STUDY

Now that you have traced Martin Industries through its benchmarking project, you should be ready to try your hand at one of your own. Ask yourself:

- What is your key business process that is most in need of improvement?
- How are you performing on the critical success factors in your business?
- Where are your competitors gaining ground on your company?
- What complaints are your customers making that indicate areas for rapid improvement?
- Have your employees made any suggestions for process improvements that have not been pursued but have a promise of performance break-throughs?

Remember, conducting a benchmarking study is of no value to your company if you have no desire to change your process behavior. This benchmarking bias to action begins with your first benchmarking action: recognizing the need for improvement and being open to change. Your exercise for this final chapter is to begin your own study. Good luck and happy benchmarking!

NOTES

1. See the MIT study cited in Chapter 6, Note 1. A basic overview of quality tools was developed by the Union of Japanese Scientists and Engineers (JUSE). This is the best introduction to quality technologies I have seen, and I recommend it for getting started on understanding and applying quality tools. The book is *TQC Solutions: The 14-Step Process*, Volumes I and II (Cambridge, Mass.: Productivity Press, 1991) and it is edited by the JUSE Problem Solving Research Group chaired by Katsuya Hosotani. Volume I provides a problem-solving process and describes the application of over 35 quality tools to this process. Volume II provides examples of the use of these tools in many different areas of a business. The only significant omissions in the applications appear to be in government and health care.

2. While there is as yet little general understanding of benchmarking, clearly there is great interest in this topic. In the October 1991 review of the Malcolm Baldrige National Quality Award criteria, there was a move to put a more explicit definition of benchmarking into the criteria as a response to the inconsistent understanding of this tool in many of the companies evaluated. In one day alone, the APQC received inquiries from over 20 companies about the International Benchmarking Clearinghouse project. The number of members who committed to assist in the design of the clearinghouse grew from a handful in May 1991 to 87 by February 1992.

Appendix

Key Business Process Matrix
Critical Success Factor Worksheet
Benchmarking Study Checklist
Business Environment Model
Process Performance Profile
Business Performance Comparison
Benchmarking Partner Analysis
Benchmarking Questionnaire
Benchmarking Action Plan
Establishing Benchmark Goals
Company Cultural Profile
Benchmarking Implementation Plan
Critical Success Factor Tracking

Key Business Process Matrix

Business Processes	Business Systems							
	Control Business	Design Products	Market Products	Purchase Materials	Produce Products	Distribute Products	Service Products	Support Business
Evaluate market information								
Develop business strategy								
Develop product requirements								
Conduct customer focus groups								
Develop customer relationships								
Perform customer surveys								
Analyze competitor performance								
Price products								
Forecast product sales								
Build prototype products								
Develop supplier relationship								
Procure and support capital equipment								
Document product design								
Plan production								
Manage incoming materials								
Assemble products								
Manage inventory								
Conduct final product test								
Package and store products								
Ship product								
Resolve customer complaints								
Perform field service								
Repair field returns								
Manage cash flow								
Evaluate and report performance								
Recruit employees								
Develop employees								
Manage and support facilities								

Relationship Strength: Strong △   Moderate ◉   Weak ○

Critical Success Factor Worksheet

Key Business Process: _____

Proposed Critical Success Factor: _____

Reason Proposed: _____

_____

CSF Process Owner: _____

_____

Analysis for CSF Qualification

1. Is the proposed CSF quantifiable?_____ How?_____

_____

_____

2. Is the proposed CSF measurable?_____ How?_____

_____

_____

3. Is the proposed CSF auditable?_____ Where?_____

_____

_____

4. Does the proposed CSF indicate process results over time?_____
   How?_____

_____

5. Does the proposed CSF indicate progress toward goal over time?_____
   How?_____

_____

6. How does a change in the key business process correlate with changes in the magnitude of
   the proposed CSF?_____

_____

_____

7. Is this measure for a proposed CSF accepted within your company?_____

_____

8. Is this proposed CSF measure widely accepted by other companies?_____
   Which companies?_____

_____

9. Is it easy to obtain data? _____ Is the data integrity reliable?_____
   Is the resulting CSF measure easily calculated? _____

_____

10. Is this proposed CSF reported in open literature?_____
    Where?_____

Benchmarking Study Checklist

Plan	
	☐ What is our process?
	☐ How does our process work?
	☐ How do we measure it?
	☐ How well is our process performing today?
	☐ Who are our customers?
	☐ What products and services do we deliver to our customers?
	☐ What do our customers expect or require of our products and services?
	☐ What is our performance goal?
	☐ How did we establish that goal?
	☐ How does our products and service performance compare with our competitors?

Search	
	☐ What companies perform this process better?
	☐ Which company is the best at performing this process?
	☐ What can we learn from that company?
	☐ Whom should we contact to determine if they are willing to participate in our study?

Observe	
	☐ What is their process?
	☐ What is their performance goal?
	☐ How well does their process perform over time and at multiple locations?
	☐ How do they measure process performance?
	☐ What enables the performance of their process?
	☐ What factors could inhibit the adaptation of their process into our company?

Analyze	
	☐ What is the nature of the performance gap?
	☐ What is the magnitude of the performance gap?
	☐ What characteristics distinguish their process as superior?
	☐ What activities within our process are candidates for change?

Adapt	
	☐ How does the knowledge of their process enable us to improve our process?
	☐ Should we redefine our performance measure or reset our performance goal based upon this benchmark?
	☐ What activities within their process would need to be modified to adapt it into our business environment?

Improve	
	☐ What have we learned during this benchmarking study that will allow us to improve upon the "superior" process?
	☐ How can we implement these changes into our process?

Business Environment Model

Competitors:

	Name	Market Share
1.	_____	_____
2.	_____	_____
3.	_____	_____
4.	_____	_____
5.	_____	_____
6.	_____	_____
7.	_____	_____

Regulatory Agencies:

	Name	Type
1.	_____	_____
2.	_____	_____
3.	_____	_____
4.	_____	_____
5.	_____	_____
6.	_____	_____
7.	_____	_____

Major Accounts:

	Name	Industry
1.	_____	_____
2.	_____	_____
3.	_____	_____
4.	_____	_____
5.	_____	_____
6.	_____	_____
7.	_____	_____

Critical Suppliers:

	Name	Technology
1.	_____	_____
2.	_____	_____
3.	_____	_____
4.	_____	_____
5.	_____	_____
6.	_____	_____
7.	_____	_____

Economic Indicators:

	Name	Value	Trend
1.	_____	_____	_____
2.	_____	_____	_____
3.	_____	_____	_____
4.	_____	_____	_____
5.	_____	_____	_____
6.	_____	_____	_____
7.	_____	_____	_____

Process Performance Profile

Process Output: _____
_____
_____
_____

Process Customer:_____
_____

Process Performance Measures:		Current Level	Trend
Quality	First-pass yield	_____	_____
	Customer returns	_____	_____
	Process completion/plan ratio	_____	_____
Cost	Process cost	_____	_____
	Process value-add	_____	_____
	Value-to-cost ratio	_____	_____
Cycle Time	Work-in-process inventory	_____	_____
	Process cycle time	_____	_____
	Process changeover time	_____	_____
	Process downtime	_____	_____

Process	Performance Goals:	Short-term	Long-term
	First pass yield	_____	_____
	Value-to-cost ratio	_____	_____
	Cycle time	_____	_____

Process Activity Diagram:

Business Performance Comparison

Measure	Company Name		
1. Return on net assets			
2. Market share			
3. Debt-equity ratio			
4. Inventory (% sales)			
5. Revenue per employee			
6. Manufacturing overhead			
7. Capital interest (% sales)			
8. R&D (% sales)			
9. R&D investment efficiency			
10. New-product cycle time			
11. Forecast cycle time			
12. Order turnaround time			
13. Material lead time			
14. Production cycle time			
15. Customer response time			
16. Customer complaints (% shipments)			
17. Field returns (% shipments)			
18. Warranty rate (% sales)			
19. Parts returned to supplier			
20. First-pass yield			

Benchmarking Partner Analysis

Measure	Company Name		
Business size:			
• sales revenue			
• number of employees			
Ownership of business			
Industry focus			
SIC code			
Organization structure			
Type of manufacturing			
Company culture:			
• formality			
• participation			
• communication			
Company competencies			

Benchmarking Questionnaire

1. How do you define this process? Please describe it.

   _____

   _____

   _____

   _____

2. Do you consider this process to be a problem or concern in your company? If not today, was it a problem in the past?

   _____

   _____

   _____

   _____

3. What is the measure of quality for this process? What are the criteria that you use to define excellence in process performance? How do you measure the output quality of this process? How do you measure progress in quality improvement?

   _____

   _____

   _____

   _____

4. How do you consider cost and schedule in this process?

   _____

   _____

   _____

   _____

5. How much and what type of training do you provide for the various job categories of the process team?

   _____

   _____

   _____

   _____

6. What process improvements have given you the best return in performance improvements?

   _____

   _____

   _____

   _____

7. What company, excluding your own, do you believe is the best in performing this process?

   _____

   _____

   _____

   _____

Benchmarking Action Plan

Process:_____

_____

Critical Success Factor: _____

_____

Process Owner: _____ **Date:**_____

Summary of Study Results

Objective

Benchmark

Company:_____

Date Observed:_____

Level:_____ Rate:_____

Goals

Short-term

Long-term

Strategy (owner)

Targets and Milestones

Establishing Benchmark Goals

Critical Success Factor: _____

Measurement Method: _____

_____

_____

Performance analysis (Top 5 Companies)   Date: _____

Company	Date	Level	Date	Level	Date	Level	Date	Goal
Self-analysis								

Best Observed Performance Level: _____

_____

Best Observed Sustained Rate of Improvement: _____

_____

Highest Stated Performance Goal: _____

_____

Recommended Short-term Goal: _____

_____

    Rationale: _____

    _____

    _____

Recommended Long-term Goal: _____

_____

    Rationale: _____

    _____

    _____

Company Cultural Profile

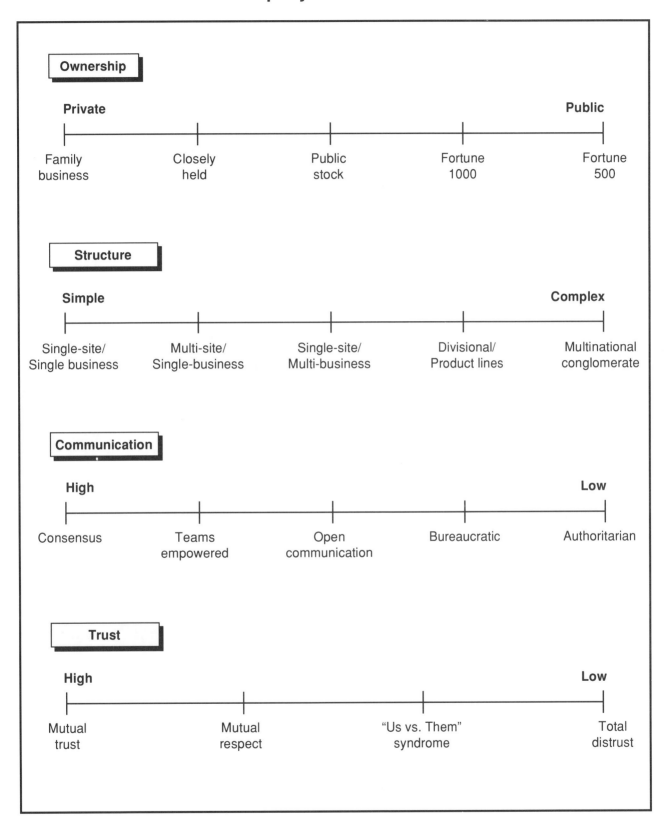

Benchmarking Implementation Plan

Process: _____

Process Owner: _____ Date: _____

Team Members: _____

_____

Strategy Statement: _____

_____

Activity	Owner	Schedule/Milestones						Performance	
		Month	Month	Month	Month	Month	Month	Target	Actual

Critical Success Factor Tracking

Critical Success Factor:	Performance			Benchmark
Location	Current level	Short-term goal Year	Long-term goal Year	Company: Date:

Performance Enablers

Short-term:

Long-term:

About the Author

Greg Watson is vice president of the Benchmarking Services at the American Productivity and Quality Center in Houston, Texas. Prior to this work with the APQC's International Benchmarking Clearinghouse, Mr. Watson was director of Corporate Quality at Compaq Computer Corporation in Houston. He managed the transition of that department from a quality-assurance organization to a customer-focused internal consulting group, created a Corporate Quality Council of senior management, led the effort to complete ISO-9002 certification at two Compaq manufacturing locations, implemented process improvement methods for activity-based cost management and just-in-time manufacturing, and developed a corporate-wide quality training curriculum.

Before joining Compaq, Mr. Watson worked with Hewlett-Packard for seven years in a number of positions, including procurement engineer, production planning manager, manufacturing improvement program manager, and quality leadership development program manager. He served as an officer in the United States Navy for 13 years, completing his service as a lieutenant commander. In the Navy, he held a variety of staff, research and development, and operational line positions.

Mr. Watson holds a bachelor of arts degree in liberal arts and chemistry from Taylor University and a master's degree in systems engineering from the University of Southern California; he has completed postgraduate studies at Stanford University in industrial engineering.

Mr. Watson is a certified quality engineer and member of the American Society for Quality Control and served as a member of the 1991 and 1992 Malcolm Baldrige National Quality Award Board of Examiners. He is a founding member of the Board of Overseers for the Texas State Quality Award and the Advisory Council of the American Productivity and Quality Center.

He is the author of a four-book set on Total Quality Management published by Productivity Press. *The Benchmarking Workbook* is the first volume, to be followed by *Benchmarking for Competitive Advantage*, *Managing by Consensus*, and *Improving Your Process* (working titles).

In the spirit of continuous improvement, the author would enjoy hearing your suggestions for improvements to this workbook. Please send any comments to Mr. Watson in care of the Editorial Department, Productivity Press, at the address on the back of the title page.

Index

MORE BOOKS ON
TOTAL QUALITY MANAGEMENT

Productivity Press publishes and distributes materials on continuous improvement in productivity, quality, customer service, and the creative involvement of all employees. Many of our products are direct source materials from Japan that have been translated into English for the first time and are available exclusively from Productivity. Supplemental products and services include newsletters, conferences, seminars, in-house training and consulting, audio-visual training programs, and industrial study missions. Call 1-800-394-8562 for our free book catalog.

Handbook of Quality Tools
The Japanese Approach

Tetsuichi Asaka and Kazuo Ozeki (eds.)

The Japanese have stunned the world by their ability to produce top quality products at competitive prices. This comprehensive teaching manual, which includes the 7 traditional and 5 newer QC tools, explains each tool, why it's useful, and how to construct and use it. Information is presented in easy-to-grasp language, with step-by-step instructions, illustrations, and examples of each tool. A perfect training aid, as well as a hands-on reference book, for supervisors, foremen, and/or team leaders. Here's the best resource on the myriad Japanese quality tools changing the face of world manufacturing today. Accessible to everyone in your organization, dealing with both management and shop floor how-to's, you'll find it an indispensable tool in your quest for quality.
ISBN 0-915299-45-3 / 336 pages / $65.00/ Order code HQT-B225

Quality Function Deployment
Integrating Customer Requirements into Product Design

Yoji Akao (ed.)

More and more, companies are using quality function deployment, or QFD, to identify their customers' requirements, translate them into quantified quality characteristics and then build them into their products and services. This casebook introduces the concept of quality deployment as it has been applied in a variety of industries in Japan. The materials include numerous case studies illustrating QFD applications. Written by the creator of QFD, this book provides direct source material on Quality Function Deployment, one of the essential tools for world class manufacturing. It is a design approach based on the idea that quality is determined by the customer. Through methodology and case studies the book offers insight into how Japanese companies identify customer requirements and describes how to translate customer requirements into qualified quality characteristics, and how to build them into products and services.
ISBN 0-915299-41-0 / 400 pages / $85.00 / Order code QFD-B225

Productivity Press, Inc., Dept. B225, P.O. Box 3007, Cambridge, MA 02140 1-800-394-6868

TQC Solutions
A 14-Step Process

JUSE Problem Solving Research Group (ed.)
Foreword by Dr. H. James Harrington

Here's a clear-cut, thoroughly explained process for putting the tools of quality control to work in your company. With a strong emphasis on the use of quality control in problem solving, this book was originally written as a handbook for the Union of Japanese Scientists and Engineers' (JUSE) renowned Quality Control seminar. Filled with practical, highly useful information, it shows you not only *how* to use the 7 QC tools, the 7 "new" QC tools, and basic statistical tools, but also suggests *when* to use them. The use of charts and matrices in problem solving is carefully examined and illustrated with examples of various problems and their solutions.
ISBN 0-915299-79-8 / 448 pages, 2 volumes / $120.00 / Order TQCS-B225

Poka-Yoke
Improving Product Quality by Preventing Defects

compiled by Nikkan Kogyo Shimbun, Ltd./Factory Magazine (ed.)
preface by Shigeo Shingo

If your goal is 100% zero defects, here is the book for you — a completely illustrated guide to poka-yoke (mistake-proofing) for supervisors and shop-floor workers. Many poka-yoke devices come from line workers and are implemented with the help of engineering staff. The result is better product quality — and greater participation by workers in efforts to improve your processes, your products, and your company as a whole.
ISBN 0-915299-31-3 / 288 pages / $65.00 / Order code IPOKA-B225

TQM for Technical Groups
Applying the Principles of Total Quality to Product Development

Kiyoshi Uchimaru, Bunteru Kurahara, and Susumu Okamoto

This practical book provides a new perspective especially for technical groups working to achieve total quality in product development. It details the application of TQM methods to product design at NEC IC Microcomputer Systems, winner of the 1987 Deming Prize and addresses the process of TQM implementation with emphasis on the role of corporate management and policy deployment *(hoshin kanri)*.
ISBN 1-56327-005-6 / 224 pages / $59.95 / Order code TQMTG-B225

Productivity Press, Inc., Dept. B225, P.O. Box 3007, Cambridge, MA 02140 1-800-394-6868

COMPLETE LIST OF TITLES FROM PRODUCTIVITY PRESS

Akao, Yoji (ed.). **Quality Function Deployment: Integrating Customer Requirements into Product Design**
ISBN 0-915299-41-0 / 1990 / 387 pages / $ 85.00 / order code QFD-B225

Akiyama, Kaneo. **Function Analysis: Systematic Improvement of Quality and Performance**
ISBN 0-915299-81-X / 1991 / 288 pages / $59.95 / order code FA-B225

Asaka, Tetsuichi and Kazuo Ozeki (eds.). **Handbook of Quality Tools: The Japanese Approach**
ISBN 0-915299-45-3 / 1990 / 336 pages / $65.00 / order code HQT-B225

Belohlav, James A. **Championship Management: An Action Model for High Performance**
ISBN 0-915299-76-3 / 1990 / 265 pages / $29.95 / order code CHAMPS-B225

Birkholz, Charles and Jim Villella. **The Battle to Stay Competitive: Changing the Traditional Workplace**
ISBN 0-915299-96-8 / 1991 / 110 pages paper / $12.00 /order code BATTLE-B225

Christopher, William F. **Productivity Measurement Handbook**
ISBN 0-915299-05-4 / 1985 / 680 pages / $150.00 / order code PMH-B225

D'Egidio, Franco. **The Service Era: Leadership in a Global Environment**
ISBN 0-915299-68-2 / 1990 / 165 pages / $29.95 / order code SERA-B225

Ford, Henry. **Today and Tomorrow**
ISBN 0-915299-36-4 / 1988 / 286 pages / $24.95 / order code FORD-B225

Fukuda, Ryuji. **CEDAC: A Tool for Continuous Systematic Improvement**
ISBN 0-915299-26-7 / 1990 / 144 pages / $54.95 / order code CEDAC-B225

Fukuda, Ryuji. **Managerial Engineering: Techniques for Improving Quality and Productivity in the Workplace** (rev.)
ISBN 0-915299-09-7 / 1986 / 208 pages / $44.95 / order code ME-B225

Gotoh, Fumio. **Equipment Planning for TPM: Maintenance Prevention Design**
ISBN 0-915299-77-1 / 1991 / 320 pages / $85.00 / order code ETPM-B225

Greif, Michel. **The Visual Factory: Building Participation Through Shared Information**
ISBN 0-915299-67-4 / 1991 / 320 pages / $54.95 / order code VFAC-B225

Hatakeyama, Yoshio. **Manager Revolution! A Guide to Survival in Today's Changing Workplace**
ISBN 0-915299-10-0 / 1986 / 208 pages / $24.95 / order code MREV-B225

Hirano, Hiroyuki. **JIT Factory Revolution: A Pictorial Guide to Factory Design of the Future**
ISBN 0-915299-44-5 / 1989 / 227 pages / $49.95 / order code JITFAC-B225

Hirano, Hiroyuki. **JIT Implementation Manual: The Complete Guide to Just-In-Time Manufacturing**
ISBN 0-915299-66-6 / 1990 / 1006 pages / $2500.00 / order code HIRJIT-B225

Horovitz, Jacques. **Winning Ways: Achieving Zero-Defect Service**
ISBN 0-915299-78-X / 1990 / 165 pages / $24.95 / order code WWAYS-B225

Ishiwata, Junichi. **IE for the Shop Floor: Productivity Through Process Analysis**
ISBN 0-915299-82-8 / 1991 / 208 pages / $39.95 / order code SHOPF1-B225

Japan Human Relations Association (ed.). **The Idea Book: Improvement Through TEI (Total Employee Involvement)**
ISBN 0-915299-22-4 / 1988 / 232 pages / $54.95 / order code IDEA-B225

Japan Human Relations Association (ed.). **The Service Industry Idea Book: Employee Involvement in Retail and Office Improvement**
ISBN 0-915299-65-8 / 1991 / 294 pages / $49.95 / order code SIDEA-B225

Japan Management Association (ed.). **Kanban and Just-In-Time at Toyota: Management Begins at the Workplace** (rev.), Translated by David J. Lu
ISBN 0-915299-48-8 / 1989 / 224 pages / $39.95 / order code KAN-B225

Productivity Press, Inc., Dept. B225, P.O. Box 3007, Cambridge, MA 02140 1-800-394-6868

Japan Management Association and Constance E. Dyer. **The Canon Production System: Creative Involvement of the Total Workforce**
ISBN 0-915299-06-2 / 1987 / 251 pages / $39.95 / order code CAN-B225

Jones, Karen (ed.). **The Best of TEI: Current Perspectives on Total Employee Involvement**
ISBN 0-915299-63-1 / 1989 / 502 pages / $199.00 / order code TEI-B225

JUSE. **TQC Solutions: The 14-Step Process**
ISBN 0-915299-79-8 / 1991 / 416 pages / 2 volumes / $120.00 / order code TQCS-B225

Kanatsu, Takashi. **TQC for Accounting: A New Role in Companywide Improvement**
ISBN 0-915299-73-9 / 1991 / 244 pages / $45.00 / order code TQCA-B225

Karatsu, Hajime. **Tough Words For American Industry**
ISBN 0-915299-25-9 / 1988 / 178 pages / $24.95 / order code TOUGH-B225

Kato, Kenichiro. **I.E. for the Shop Floor: Productivity Through Motion Study**
ISBN 1-56327-000-5 / 1991 / 224 pages / $39.95 / order code SHOPF2-B225

Kaydos, Will. **Measuring, Managing, and Maximizing Performance**
ISBN 0-915299-98-4 / 1991 / 304 pages / $39.95 / order code MMMP-B225

Kobayashi, Iwao. **20 Keys to Workplace Improvement**
ISBN 0-915299-61-5 / 1990 / 264 pages / $39.95 / order code 20KEYS-B225

Lu, David J. **Inside Corporate Japan: The Art of Fumble-Free Management**
ISBN 0-915299-16-X / 1987 / 278 pages / $24.95 / order code ICJ-B225

Maskell, Brain H. **Performance Measurement for World Class Manufacturing: A Model for American Companies**
ISBN 0-915299-99-2 / 1991 / 448 pages / $54.95 / order code PERFM-B225

Merli, Giorgio. **Co-makership: The New Supply Strategy for Manufacturers**
ISBN 0-915299-84-4 / 1991 / 224 pages / $39.95 / order code COMAKE-B225

Merli, Giorgio. **Total Manufacturing Management: Production Organization for the 1990s**
ISBN 0-915299-58-5 / 1990 / 304 pages / $39.95 / order code TMM-B225

Mizuno, Shigeru (ed.). **Management for Quality Improvement: The 7 New QC Tools**
ISBN 0-915299-29-1 / 1988 / 324 pages / $65.00 / order code 7QC-B225

Monden, Yasuhiro and Michiharu Sakurai (eds.). **Japanese Management Accounting: A World Class Approach to Profit Management**
ISBN 0-915299-50-X / 1990 / 568 pages / $65.00 / order code JMACT-B225

Nachi-Fujikoshi (ed.). **Training for TPM: A Manufacturing Success Story**
ISBN 0-915299-34-8 / 1990 / 272 pages / $65.00 / order code CTPM-B225

Nakajima, Seiichi. **Introduction to TPM: Total Productive Maintenance**
ISBN 0-915299-23-2 / 1988 / 149 pages / $45.00 / order code ITPM-B225

Nakajima, Seiichi. **TPM Development Program: Implementing Total Productive Maintenance**
ISBN 0-915299-37-2 / 1989 / 428 pages / $95.00 / order code DTPM-B225

Nikkan Kogyo Shimbun, Ltd./Factory Magazine (ed.). **Poka-yoke: Improving Product Quality by Preventing Defects**
ISBN 0-915299-31-3 / 1989 / 288 pages / $65.00 / order code IPOKA-B225

Nikkan Kogyo Shimbun/Esme McTighe (ed.). **Factory Management Notebook Series: Mixed Model Production**
ISBN 0-915299-97-6 / 1991 / 184 pages / $95.00 / order code N1-MM-B225

Nikkan Kogyo Shimbun/Esme McTighe (ed.). **Factory Management Notebook Series: Visual Control Systems**
ISBN 0-915299-54-2 / 1991 / 194 pages / $95.00 / order code N1-VCS-B225

Productivity Press, Inc., Dept. B225, P.O. Box 3007, Cambridge, MA 02140 1-800-394-6868

Nikkan Kogyo Shimbun/Esme McTighe (ed.). **Factory Management Notebook Series: Autonomation/ Automation**
ISBN 0-56327-002-1 / 1991 / 200 pages / $95.00 / order code N1-AA-B225

Ohno, Taiichi. **Toyota Production System: Beyond Large-Scale Production**
ISBN 0-915299-14-3 / 1988 / 162 pages / $42.95 / order code OTPS-B225

Ohno, Taiichi. **Workplace Management**
ISBN 0-915299-19-4 / 1988 / 165 pages / $39.95 / order code WPM-B225

Ohno, Taiichi and Setsuo Mito. **Just-In-Time for Today and Tomorrow**
ISBN 0-915299-20-8 / 1988 / 208 pages / $39.95 / order code OMJIT-B225

Perigord, Michel. **Achieving Total Quality Management: A Program for Action**
ISBN 0-915299-60-7 / 1991 / 384 pages / $49.95 / order code ACHTQM-B225

Psarouthakis, John. **Better Makes Us Best**
ISBN 0-915299-56-9 / 1989 / 112 pages / $16.95 / order code BMUB-B225

Robinson, Alan. **Continuous Improvement in Operations: A Systematic Approach to Waste Reduction**
ISBN 0-915299-51-8 / 1991 / 416 pages / $34.95 / order code ROB2-C-B225

Robson, Ross (ed.). T**he Quality and Productivity Equation: American Corporate Strategies for the 1990s**
ISBN 0-915299-71-2 / 1990 / 558 pages / $29.95 / order code QPE-B225

Shetty, Y.K and Vernon M. Buehler (eds.). **Competing Through Productivity and Quality**
ISBN 0-915299-43-7 / 1989 / 576 pages / $39.95 / order code COMP-B225

Shingo, Shigeo. **Non-Stock Production: The Shingo System for Continuous Improvement**
ISBN 0-915299-30-5 / 1988 / 480 pages / $85.00 / order code NON-B225

Shingo, Shigeo. **A Revolution In Manufacturing: The SMED System**, Translated by Andrew P. Dillon
ISBN 0-915299-03-8 / 1985 / 383 pages / $75.00 / order code SMED-B225

Shingo, Shigeo. **The Sayings of Shigeo Shingo: Key Strategies for Plant Improvement**, Translated by Andrew P. Dillon
ISBN 0-915299-15-1 / 1987 / 208 pages / $44.95 / order code SAY-B225

Shingo, Shigeo. **A Study of the Toyota Production System from an Industrial Engineering Viewpoint**
ISBN 0-915299-17-8 / 1989 / 293 pages / $44.95 / order code STREV-B225

Shingo, Shigeo. **Zero Quality Control: Source Inspection and the Poka-yoke System**,Translated by Andrew P. Dillon
ISBN 0-915299-07-0 / 1986 / 328 pages / $75.00 / order code ZQC-B225

Shinohara, Isao (ed.). **New Production System: JIT Crossing Industry Boundaries**
ISBN 0-915299-21-6 / 1988 / 224 pages / $39.95 / order code NPS-B225

Sugiyama, Tomo. **The Improvement Book: Creating the Problem-Free Workplace**
ISBN 0-915299-47-X / 1989 / 236 pages / $54.95 / order code IB-B225

Suzue, Toshio and Akira Kohdate. **Variety Reduction Program (VRP): A Production Strategy for Product Diversification**
ISBN 0-915299-32-1 / 1990 / 164 pages / $59.95 / order code VRP-B225

Tateisi, Kazuma. **The Eternal Venture Spirit: An Executive's Practical Philosophy**
ISBN 0-915299-55-0 / 1989 / 208 pages/ $19.95 / order code EVS-B225

Yasuda, Yuzo. **40 Years, 20 Million Ideas: The Toyota Suggestion System**
ISBN 0-915299-74-7 / 1991 / 210 pages / $39.95 / order code 4020-B225

Productivity Press, Inc., Dept. B225, P.O. Box 3007, Cambridge, MA 02140 1-800-394-6868

Audio-Visual Programs

Japan Management Association. **Total Productive Maintenance: Maximizing Productivity and Quality**
ISBN 0-915299-46-1 / 167 slides / 1989 / $799.00 / order code STPM-B225
ISBN 0-915299-49-6 / 2 videos / 1989 / $799.00 / order code VTPM-B225

Shingo, Shigeo. **The SMED System**, Translated by Andrew P. Dillon
ISBN 0-915299-11-9 / 181 slides / 1986 / $799.00 / order code S5-B225
ISBN 0-915299-27-5 / 2 videos / 1987 / $799.00 / order code V5-B225

Shingo, Shigeo. **The Poka-yoke System**, Translated by Andrew P. Dillon
ISBN 0-915299-13-5 / 235 slides / 1987 / $799.00 / order code S6-B225
ISBN 0-915299-28-3 / 2 videos / 1987 / $799.00 / order code V6-B225

Returns of AV programs willl be accepted for incorrect or damaged shipments only.

TO ORDER: Write, phone, or fax Productivity Press, Dept. BK, P.O. Box 3007, Cambridge, MA 02140, phone 1-800-274-9911, fax 617-864-6286. Send check or charge to your credit card (American Express, Visa, MasterCard accepted).

U.S. ORDERS: Add $5 shipping for first book, $2 each additional for UPS surface delivery. CT residents add 8% and MA residents 5% sales tax. For each AV program that you order, add $5 for programs with 1 or 2 tapes, and $12 for programs with 3 or more tapes.

INTERNATIONAL ORDERS: Write, phone, or fax for quote and indicate shipping method desired. Pre-payment in U.S. dollars must accompany your order (checks must be drawn on U.S. banks). When quote is returned with payment, your order will be shipped promptly by the method requested.

NOTE: Prices subject to change without notice.

Productivity Press, Inc., Dept. B225, P.O. Box 3007, Cambridge, MA 02140 1-800-394-6868